New Ways With
MINCE

Food SHERYLE EASTWOOD
Styling DONNA HAY
Photography QUENTIN BACON

A J.B. Fairfax Press Publication

INTRODUCTION

The wonderful recipes and ideas in this book for preparing and serving mince are sure to impress family and friends. Mince is a popular, economic and without doubt the most versatile form of meat. Just think of what you can do with it – roll or shape it, then poach, bake, pan cook, stir-fry or even roast it.

Supermarkets and butchers, recognising the popularity of mince, plus the fact that many people are becoming increasing health-conscious, are now producing low-fat or slimmer's mince. This is a boon for the family slimmer and those who are generally concerned about what they and their families are eating. The recipes in this book use lean mince, however they are just as delicious made with standard mince.

UK COOKERY EDITOR
Katie Swallow

EDITORIAL
Food Editor: Rachel Blackmore
Editorial and Production Assistant: Sheridan Packer
Editorial Coordinator: Margaret Kelly
Recipe Development: Sheryle Eastwood

Photography: Quentin Bacon
Step photography: William Meppem
Styling: Donna Hay
Food Stylist's Assistant: Jody Vassallo

DESIGN AND PRODUCTION
Managers: Sheridan Carter, Anna Maguire
Layout and Design: Lulu Dougherty
Cover Design: Frank Pithers

Published by J.B. Fairfax Press Pty Limited
A.C.N. 003 738 430

Formatted by J.B. Fairfax Press Pty Limited
Printed by Toppan Printing Co, Hong Kong

JBFP 302 UK
Includes Index
ISBN 1 86343 141 1

Distributed by J.B. Fairfax Press Ltd
9 Trinity Centre, Park Farm Estate
Wellingborough, Nothants, United Kingdom
Ph: (0933) 402330 Fax: (0933) 402234

THE PANTRY SHELF

Unless otherwise stated, the following ingredients used in this book are:

Cream	Double, suitable for whipping
Flour	White flour, plain or standard
Sugar	White sugar

WHAT'S IN A TABLESPOON?

AUSTRALIA
1 tablespoon = 20 mL OR 4 teaspoons

NEW ZEALAND
1 tablespoon = 15 mL OR 3 teaspoons

UNITED KINGDOM
1 tablespoon = 15 mL OR 3 teaspoons

The recipes in this book were tested in Australia where a 20 mL tablespoon is standard. All measures are level.

The tablespoon in the New Zealand and United Kingdom sets of measuring spoons is 15 mL. For recipes using baking powder, gelatine, bicarbonate of soda, small quantities of flour and cornflour, simply add another teaspoon for each tablespoon specified.

CANNED FOOD

Can sizes vary between countries and manufacturers. You may find the quantities in this book are slightly different from what is available. Purchase and use the can size nearest to the suggested size in the recipe.

MICROWAVE IT

Where microwave instructions occur in this book a microwave oven with a 650 watt output has been used. Wattage on domestic microwave ovens varies between 500 and 700 watts, so it may be necessary to vary cooking times slightly depending on the wattage of your oven.

Contents

RECIPE COLLECTION

EXOTIC FLAVOURS

Many of the tastiest and most popular minced meat dishes have their origins in foreign countries. The recipes in this chapter have an exotic influence and yet remind you of minced meat's versatility.

SAMOSA FLANS WITH SAMBAL

Oven temperature
200°C, 400°F, Gas 6

This is a great do ahead dish. Make pastry cases several days in advance and store in an airtight container or freeze for a longer period. Make the filling and sambal up to a day in advance and store it covered in the refrigerator. Just prior to serving, reheat the pastry cases in the oven for 5 minutes, and the filling in the microwave or in a saucepan over a medium heat until hot.

375 g/12 oz prepared shortcrust pastry
2 teaspoons desiccated coconut

SPICY FILLING
15 g/$^{1}/_{2}$ oz ghee or 1 tablespoon vegetable oil
1 onion, finely chopped
2 cloves garlic, crushed
1 teaspoon finely grated fresh ginger
$^{1}/_{2}$ teaspoon ground cumin
$^{1}/_{2}$ teaspoon ground cinnamon
$^{1}/_{4}$ teaspoon ground cloves
$^{1}/_{4}$ teaspoon ground cardamom
1 teaspoon curry paste (vindaloo)
375 g/12 oz lean beef mince
1 potato, cubed
$^{1}/_{4}$ cup/60 mL/2 fl oz beef stock
2 tablespoons coconut milk
1 tablespoon finely chopped fresh coriander

TOMATO SAMBAL
1 large tomato, finely chopped
1 small green or red chilli, finely chopped
2 teaspoons lemon juice
1 red onion, finely chopped
1 tablespoon chopped fresh mint

1 Roll out pastry and line eight 10 cm/4 in flan tins. Line pastry cases with nonstick baking paper, fill with uncooked rice and bake for 10 minutes. Remove rice and paper from pastry cases and bake for 5 minutes longer or until pastry is golden.

2 To make filling, melt ghee or heat oil in a frying pan over a medium heat, add onion and cook for 3-4 minutes or until soft. Stir in garlic, ginger, cumin, cinnamon, cloves, cardamom and curry paste (vindaloo) and cook for 2 minutes. Add beef and cook, stirring, until meat is brown. Reduce heat to low, add potato, stock and coconut milk and cook, stirring occasionally, for 10-15 minutes or until potato is soft. Stir in coriander.

3 To make sambal, combine tomato, chilli, lemon juice, onion and mint.

4 To serve, divide filling between warm pastry cases, top with a spoonful of sambal and sprinkle with coconut.

Serves 4

Samosa Flans with Sambal

Burritos with Avocado Mayonnaise

Oven temperature
150°C, 300°F, Gas 2

1 tablespoon vegetable oil
1 onion, finely chopped
500 g/1 lb lean beef mince
30 g/1 oz packet chilli seasoning mix
1/2 cup/125 mL/4 fl oz bottled tomato salsa
440 g/14 oz canned tomatoes, undrained and mashed
1/2 cup/125 mL/4 fl oz beef stock
315 g/10 oz canned red kidney beans, drained and rinsed
8 tortillas
90 g/3 oz butter, melted
1 red pepper, cut into strips

AVOCADO MAYONNAISE

1 large avocado, peeled and seeded
1/2 cup/125 g/4 oz sour cream
1/4 cup/60 mL/2 fl oz cream (double)
2 teaspoons lemon juice
1 tablespoon mayonnaise
pinch chilli powder

1 Heat oil in a frying pan over a medium heat, add onion and cook for 3-4 minutes or until soft. Add beef and cook, stirring, until meat is brown. Stir in seasoning mix, salsa, tomatoes, stock and beans and bring to the boil. Reduce heat and simmer for 20 minutes or until mixture thickens slightly. Remove pan from heat and set aside to cool.

2 Brush tortillas with butter and stack on a greased 30 x 60 cm/12 x 24 in piece of aluminium foil. Wrap tortillas tightly in foil and bake for 15 minutes.

3 Spoon meat mixture into the centre of each tortilla. Fold tortilla like an envelope to form a parcel and place seam side down in a shallow ovenproof dish. Brush with butter and bake at 180°C/ 350°F/Gas 4 for 15 minutes or until heated through.

4 To make mayonnaise, place avocado, sour cream, cream, lemon juice, mayonnaise and chilli powder in a food processor or blender and process until smooth.

5 To serve, spoon mayonnaise over hot burritos and top with red pepper strips.

Serves 8

A favourite Mexican dish, these burritos are sure to be just as popular in your house as they are in their country of origin. Tortillas are available from speciality food shops and most supermarkets.

Nasi Goreng

CHILLI MEATBALLS
250 g/8 oz lean beef mince
1 onion, finely chopped
1/2 teaspoon minced red chilli
1/2 teaspoon curry paste (vindaloo)
1 egg white, lightly beaten
vegetable oil for deep-frying

NASI GORENG RICE
2 eggs, lightly beaten
1 tablespoon soy sauce
1/4 cup/60 mL/2 fl oz peanut (groundnut) oil
2 onions, thinly sliced
2 cloves garlic, crushed
1/2 red pepper, chopped
1/2 green pepper, chopped
1 teaspoon minced red chilli
1 boneless chicken breast fillet, chopped
1 x 375 g/12 oz fillet pork, chopped
250 g/8 oz uncooked prawns, shelled and deveined
125 g/4 oz bean sprouts
2 1/4 cups/500 g/1 lb long grain rice, cooked
1 tablespoon chopped fresh coriander

In this version of a traditional Indonesian dish chicken or pork mince are delicious alternatives for the meatballs.

1 To make meatballs, place beef, onion, chilli, curry paste (vindaloo) and egg white in a bowl and mix to combine. Shape meat mixture into small balls.

2 Heat vegetable oil in a large saucepan until a cube of bread dropped in browns in 50 seconds. Cook meatballs a few at a time for 4-5 minutes or until golden and cooked through. Drain meatballs on absorbent kitchen paper, then thread onto short bamboo skewers, set aside and keep warm.

3 For rice, place eggs and 1 teaspoon soy sauce in a bowl and whisk to combine. Heat 1 tablespoon peanut (groundnut) oil in a heavy-based frying pan over a medium heat, add egg mixture and cook, without stirring, until set. Remove omelette from pan, cut half into small pieces and half into long strips. Set aside.

4 Heat remaining peanut (groundnut) oil in frying pan over a medium heat, add onions, garlic, red pepper and green pepper and stir-fry for 3-4 minutes or until onion is soft. Add chilli, chicken and pork and stir-fry for 8-10 minutes longer or until meat is brown.

5 Add prawns, bean sprouts and rice and stir-fry for 4-5 minutes or until mixture is heated through. Stir in coriander, chopped omelette and remaining soy sauce and stir-fry for 1-2 minutes longer.

6 To serve, spoon rice into the centre of a serving platter, top with omelette strips and surround with skewered meatballs.

Serves 6

Nasi Goreng

Chilli Con Carne

Chilli Con Carne

1 tablespoon olive oil
1 onion, finely chopped
2 cloves garlic, crushed
1 green pepper, chopped
500 g/1 lb lean beef mince
2 teaspoons ground paprika
1/2 teaspoon chilli powder
1/2 teaspoon ground cumin
1 teaspoon minced red chilli
440 g/14 oz canned tomato purée (passata)
1/2 cup/125 mL/4 fl oz beef stock
1/2 cup/125 mL/4 fl oz red wine
315 g/10 oz canned red kidney beans, drained and rinsed
freshly ground black pepper
vegetable oil for deep-frying
4 tortillas
1/2 cup/125 g/4 oz sour cream

1 Heat olive oil in a frying pan over a medium heat, add onion, garlic and green pepper and cook, stirring, for 3-4 minutes or until onion is soft. Stir in beef and cook for 5 minutes or until meat is brown.

2 Add paprika, chilli powder, cumin, chilli, tomato purée (passata), stock and wine to meat mixture, bring to simmering and simmer, stirring occasionally, for 25 minutes or until liquid is reduced by half. Stir in beans and black pepper to taste and cook for 10 minutes longer.

3 Heat vegetable oil in a large saucepan until a cube of bread dropped in browns in 50 seconds. Cook tortillas one at a time, pushing down with a small ladle, to make a basket shape, for 3-4 minutes or until golden. Drain on absorbent kitchen paper. Spoon meat mixture into tortilla baskets and top with sour cream.

Serves 4

Another easy serving idea for this spicy meat mixture is to spoon it over hot baked potatoes. Cook four large potatoes in the oven at 200°C/400°F/Gas 6 for 1 hour or the microwave on HIGH (100%) for 15 minutes or until tender. Cut a cross in the top of the potatoes and using a clean cloth push up. Spoon meat mixture over potatoes and top with sour cream.

RECIPE COLLECTION

Moussaka-filled Shells

Oven temperature
180°C, 350°F, Gas 4

The tomato supreme used in this recipe consists of tomatoes, celery, peppers and various spices, if it is unavailable use canned tomatoes instead.

2 large eggplant (aubergines)
salt
olive oil
45 g/1 1/2 oz grated Parmesan cheese
30 g/1 oz butter

MEAT SAUCE
1 onion, finely chopped
1 clove garlic, crushed
500 g/1 lb lean lamb mince
315 g/10 oz canned tomato supreme
1/2 cup/125 mL/4 fl oz dry white wine
1/2 cup/125 mL/4 fl oz chicken stock
2 tablespoons finely chopped fresh basil
1 tablespoon finely chopped fresh parsley
freshly ground black pepper

CHEESE SAUCE
60 g/2 oz butter
1/4 cup/30 g/1 oz flour
1/4 teaspoon ground nutmeg
1 cup/250 mL/8 fl oz milk
1/2 cup/125 g/4 oz sour cream
125 g/4 oz tasty cheese (mature Cheddar), grated

EGGPLANT (AUBERGINE) PUREE
reserved eggplant (aubergine) flesh
1 clove garlic, crushed
1 small onion, grated
3 tablespoons chopped fresh parsley
2 tablespoons lemon juice

1 Cut eggplant (aubergines) in half, lengthwise. Scoop out flesh leaving a 5 mm/1/4 in shell. Chop flesh and reserve to make the purée. Sprinkle eggplant (aubergine) shells with salt, turn upside down and set aside to stand for 20 minutes. Rinse shells under cold running water and pat dry. Brush eggplant (aubergine) shells inside and out with olive oil and place on a baking tray.

2 To make Meat Sauce, heat 1 tablespoon olive oil in a nonstick frying pan over a medium heat, add onion and garlic and cook, stirring, for 2-3 minutes or until onion is soft. Stir in lamb and cook until meat is brown. Add tomato supreme, wine, stock, basil, parsley and black pepper to taste to pan, bring to simmering and simmer for 25 minutes or until mixture reduces and thickens.

3 To make Cheese Sauce, melt butter in a saucepan over a medium heat. Add flour and nutmeg and cook, stirring, for 3 minutes. Remove pan from heat and whisk in milk and sour cream. Return pan to heat and cook, stirring, for 3-4 minutes or until sauce boils and thickens. Remove pan from heat and stir in cheese.

4 Divide Meat Sauce between eggplant (aubergine) shells, top with Cheese Sauce, sprinkle with Parmesan cheese and dot with butter. Bake for 20-25 minutes or until filling is hot and bubbling and top is golden.

5 To make purée, place reserved eggplant (aubergine) flesh, 1/4 cup/60 mL/2 fl oz olive oil, garlic and onion in a nonstick frying pan and cook over a medium heat, stirring, for 4-5 minutes or until eggplant (aubergine) is soft. Place eggplant (aubergine) mixture, parsley, lemon juice and black pepper to taste in a food processor or blender and process until smooth. Serve with Moussaka-filled Shells.

Serves 4

Spanish Meatball Soup

125 g/4 oz lean beef mince
2 cloves garlic, crushed
3 tablespoons toasted pine nuts
1 tablespoon chopped fresh parsley
2 teaspoons dry sherry
1 tablespoon flour
freshly ground black pepper
vegetable oil for deep-frying
60 g/2 oz butter
1 large carrot, sliced
1 stalk celery, sliced
1 onion, chopped
1 large potato, diced
440 g/14 oz canned tomatoes, undrained and mashed
4 cups/1 litre/1$^3/_4$ pt beef stock
1 chorizo sausage, sliced

Serves 4

1 Place beef, garlic, pine nuts, parsley, sherry, flour and black pepper to taste in a bowl and mix to combine. Shape mixture into small meatballs.

2 Heat oil in a large saucepan until a cube of bread dropped in browns in 50 seconds. Cook meatballs in batches for 3-4 minutes or until golden. Drain on absorbent kitchen paper and set aside.

3 Melt butter in a large saucepan, add carrot, celery, onion and potato, cover and cook over a low heat, stirring occasionally, for 5 minutes.

4 Stir tomatoes and stock into vegetable mixture and bring to the boil. Reduce heat, add meatballs and sausage and simmer for 20-25 minutes.

Chorizo sausage is a spicy sausage of Spanish origin. It has a coarse dry texture and its predominant ingredients are pork and red pepper. Use any spicy sausage or salami instead if you wish.

Spanish Meat Omelette

$^1/_3$ cup/90 mL/3 fl oz olive oil
1 large onion, finely chopped
1 red pepper, finely chopped
500 g/1 lb lean beef mince
$^1/_2$ beef stock cube
$^1/_2$ teaspoon ground allspice
1 teaspoon ground cumin
3 tablespoons snipped fresh chives
freshly ground black pepper
1 large potato, cooked and mashed
6 eggs, lightly beaten
125 g/4 oz grated tasty cheese (mature Cheddar)

Serves 6

1 Heat 2 tablespoons oil in a heavy-based frying pan, add onion and red pepper and cook for 3-4 minutes or until onion is soft. Add beef and cook, stirring, for 5 minutes. Stir in stock cube, allspice, cumin, chives and black pepper to taste and cook for 2-3 minutes longer.

2 Place meat mixture, potato, eggs and half the cheese in a bowl and mix to combine.

3 Heat remaining oil in a clean frying pan over a low heat, pour in meat mixture, sprinkle with remaining cheese, cover and cook for 20 minutes or until omelette is set. Place pan under a preheated hot grill and cook for 3-4 minutes or until top is golden.

Beef mince is used in this recipe, however you may prefer to try chicken or pork; both are delicious alternatives.

Spanish Meat Omelette, Spanish Meatball Soup

Hungarian Pork Slice

Oven temperature
180°C, 350°F, Gas 4

1/2 large cabbage, leaves separated
1 tablespoon vegetable oil
1 onion, chopped
2 cloves garlic, crushed
500 g/1 lb lean pork mince
1/3 cup/75 g/2 1/2 oz short grain rice, cooked
3/4 cup/45 g/1 1/2 oz breadcrumbs, made from stale bread
1/2 cup/125 mL/4 fl oz milk
1/2 teaspoon dried marjoram
1/4 teaspoon caraway seeds
1 tablespoon ground paprika
2 eggs, lightly beaten
freshly ground black pepper
4 rashers bacon, rind removed

SOUR CREAM SAUCE
30 g/1 oz butter
1 tablespoon flour
1/2 cup/125 mL/4 fl oz chicken stock
1/2 cup/125 g/4 oz sour cream

1 Boil or microwave cabbage leaves until tender. Drain, refresh under cold water and drain again. Line a greased, shallow ovenproof dish with some of the cabbage leaves. Set remaining leaves aside.

2 Heat oil in a frying pan, add onion and garlic and cook until onion is soft. Cool. Combine pork, rice, breadcrumbs, milk, marjoram, caraway seeds, paprika, eggs, black pepper to taste and onion mixture.

3 Spoon half the pork mixture into cabbage-lined dish, top with a layer of cabbage leaves and the remaining pork. Arrange bacon over top, cover and bake for 1 hour or until cooked. Drain off cooking juices and reserve.

4 To make sauce, melt butter in a saucepan over a low heat, add flour and cook, stirring, for 2-3 minutes. Remove pan from heat and whisk in stock and reserved cooking juices. Return pan to heat and cook, stirring constantly, for 3-4 minutes or until sauce boils and thickens. Remove pan from heat and whisk in sour cream and black pepper to taste. To serve, invert slice onto a serving plate, cut into wedges and accompany with sauce.

Serves 4

This slice is delicious served hot, warm or cold. Cold it is perfect in packed lunches or as part of a picnic feast. If serving it cold you may prefer to accompany the slice with a tasty tomato sauce.

Chilli Beef Tacos

A quick and tasty dish that only requires a tossed green salad to make a complete meal. This dish is ideal for those occasions when you have family eating at different times. The Meat Sauce and tacos reheat well in the microwave. In the microwave 2 taco shells will take 30 seconds to heat on HIGH (100%).

8 taco shells, warmed
1 avocado, peeled and finely chopped
1/2 cup/125 mL/4 fl oz bottled tomato salsa
125 g/4 oz grated tasty cheese (mature Cheddar)

MEAT SAUCE
1 tablespoon olive oil
30 g/1 oz butter
1 onion, finely chopped
2 cloves garlic, crushed
2 small fresh red chillies, finely chopped
2 teaspoons ground cumin
1 tablespoon ground paprika
500 g/1 lb lean beef mince
440 g/14 oz canned tomatoes, undrained and mashed
1/2 cup/125 mL/4 fl oz bottled tomato salsa
2 tablespoons tomato paste (purée)
315 g/10 oz canned red kidney beans, drained and rinsed

1 To make sauce, heat oil and butter in a frying pan, add onion, garlic, chillies, cumin and paprika and cook over a medium heat, stirring, for 2-3 minutes or until onion is soft.

2 Stir in beef and cook for 5 minutes or until meat is brown. Add tomatoes, salsa and tomato paste (purée) to pan, bring to the boil, then reduce heat and simmer for 15-20 minutes, or until mixture reduces and thickens slightly. Stir in beans and cook for 5 minutes longer.

3 Divide sauce between taco shells, top with avocado, salsa and cheese. Serve immediately.

Serves 4

San Choy Bow

While pork is the traditional meat used in this Oriental dish, it is also tasty made with other varieties of mince, beef, lamb, chicken and turkey are all good alternatives.

90 g/3 oz dried Chinese mushrooms
1 tablespoon peanut (groundnut) oil
500 g/1 lb lean pork mince
125 g/4 oz cooked medium prawns, shelled, deveined and halved
3 tablespoons unsalted peanuts, toasted
125 g/4 oz canned water chestnuts, drained and chopped
125 g/4 oz canned bamboo shoots, drained and chopped
1/2 teaspoon sesame oil
1 tablespoon soy sauce
2 teaspoons oyster sauce
2 tablespoons dry sherry
8 lettuce cups

1 Place mushrooms in a bowl and cover with boiling water. Soak for 20 minutes or until tender. Drain and chop mushrooms.

2 Heat peanut (groundnut) oil in a wok or large frying pan, add pork and stir-fry until brown. Add prawns and peanuts and stir-fry for 2-3 minutes longer. Stir in mushrooms, water chestnuts, bamboo shoots, sesame oil, soy sauce, oyster sauce and sherry and mix to combine.

3 To serve, spoon pork mixture into the centre of a large serving platter and surround with lettuce cups. To eat, each person places some of the pork mixture in a lettuce cup, then rolls it up and eats it.

Serves 4

Pastitsio

250 g/8 oz fettuccine
250 g/8 oz ricotta cheese, drained
1 egg, lightly beaten
1/4 teaspoon ground nutmeg
1 tablespoon olive oil
1 onion, finely chopped
500 g/1 lb lean beef mince
440 g/14 oz canned tomatoes, undrained and mashed
1 tablespoon tomato paste (purée)
1 cup/250 mL/8 fl oz beef stock
1 teaspoon dried oregano
2 tablespoons chopped fresh parsley
freshly ground black pepper

CHEESY TOPPING
60 g/2 oz butter
1/4 cup/30 g/1 oz flour
2 cups/500 mL/16 fl oz milk
1/2 cup/125 mL/4 fl oz cream (double)
1/4 teaspoon ground nutmeg
2 eggs, lightly beaten
125 g/4 oz grated Romano or Parmesan cheese
2 tablespoons breadcrumbs, made from stale bread

1 Cook pasta in boiling water in a large saucepan following packet directions. Drain well and place in a large bowl. Add ricotta cheese, egg and nutmeg and mix well to combine. Press pasta mixture into a greased shallow ovenproof dish.

2 Heat oil in a large frying pan over a medium heat, add onion and cook for 2-3 minutes, or until soft. Add beef and cook, stirring, for 5 minutes or until meat is brown. Stir in tomatoes, tomato paste (purée), stock, oregano, parsley and black pepper to taste and bring to the boil. Reduce heat and simmer for 20-25 minutes or until sauce reduces and thickens. Spoon meat mixture over pasta and set aside.

3 To make topping, melt butter in a saucepan over a medium heat, stir in flour and cook, stirring constantly, for 2 minutes. Remove pan from heat and gradually whisk in milk and cream. Return pan to heat and cook over a medium heat, stirring constantly, until mixture boils and thickens. Remove pan from heat and whisk in nutmeg, eggs and Romano or Parmesan cheese. Spoon sauce over meat mixture, sprinkle with breadcrumbs and bake for 35-40 minutes or until top is lightly browned. Stand for 15 minutes before serving.

Serves 6

Oven temperature
180°C, 350°F, Gas 4

Pastitsio is the Greek version of a baked pasta and beef casserole. It makes a pleasant alternative to lasagne and only requires a tossed green salad or a sauté of vegetables to accompany it.

Pastitsio

Spring Roll Baskets

vegetable oil for deep-frying
8 spring roll or wonton wrappers, each 12.5 cm/5 in square
2 tablespoons unsalted cashews, toasted and chopped

PORK AND PRAWN FILLING
1 tablespoon peanut (groundnut) oil
2 teaspoons finely grated fresh ginger
1 small fresh red chilli, finely chopped
4 spring onions, finely chopped
250 g/8 oz lean pork mince
125 g/4 oz uncooked prawns, shelled and deveined
1 tablespoon soy sauce
2 teaspoons fish sauce
2 teaspoons honey
2 teaspoons lemon juice
30 g/1 oz bean sprouts
1 small carrot, cut into thin strips
1 tablespoon finely chopped fresh coriander

1 Heat vegetable oil in a large saucepan until a cube of bread dropped in browns in 50 seconds. Place 2 spring roll or wonton wrappers, diagonally, one on top of the other, so that the corners are not matching. Shape wrappers around the base of a small ladle, lower into hot oil and cook for 3-4 minutes. During cooking keep wrappers submerged in oil by pushing down with the ladle to form a basket shape. Drain on absorbent kitchen paper. Repeat with remaining wrappers to make four baskets.

2 To make filling, heat peanut (groundnut) oil in a frying pan, add ginger, chilli and spring onions and stir-fry for 1 minute. Add pork and stir-fry for 5 minutes or until meat is brown. Add prawns, soy sauce, fish sauce, honey, lemon juice, bean sprouts, carrot and coriander and stir-fry for 4-5 minutes longer or until prawns change colour.

3 To serve, spoon filling into baskets and sprinkle with cashews.

Serves 4

Wonton or spring roll wrappers are available frozen from Asian food shops and some supermarkets.

MEATLOAVES

Meatloaf is an all-time family favourite, but with this selection of recipes you will no longer keep it just for the family.

LAMB AND KIDNEY LOAF

Oven temperature
180°C, 350°F, Gas 4

Meatloaves are great when feeding a crowd and most are just as good cold as they are hot. Next time you are having a party why not serve a selection of cold meatloaves. Make them the day before and chill overnight; prior to serving cut the meatloaves into slices and arrange on beds of lettuce on large serving platters. Accompany with a selection of salads, mustards, chutneys and relishes and some crusty bread for a meal that is sure to appeal to all age groups.

3 lamb kidneys, trimmed of all visible fat
3 bay leaves
6 rashers bacon, rind removed
30 g/1 oz butter
1 onion, finely chopped
1/4 cup/60 mL/2 fl oz brandy
1 tablespoon finely chopped fresh thyme or 1 teaspoon dried thyme
1 tablespoon green peppercorns in brine, drained
750 g/1 1/2 lb lean lamb mince
3/4 cup/45 g/1 1/2 oz breadcrumbs, made from stale bread
1/2 chicken stock cube
1 tablespoon tomato paste (purée)
1 egg, lightly beaten

GREEN PEPPERCORN SAUCE
2 tablespoons brown sugar
30 g/1 oz butter
1/4 cup/60 mL/2 fl oz red wine
2 tablespoons brandy
1 cup/250 mL/8 fl oz chicken stock
2 teaspoons green peppercorns in brine, drained
1/2 cup/125 mL/4 fl oz cream (double)

1 Soak kidneys in a bowl of salted water for 10 minutes. Drain, then pat dry with absorbent kitchen paper. Cut into slices, discarding core and set aside.

2 Arrange bay leaves in the base of a greased 11 x 21 cm/4 1/2 x 8 1/2 in loaf tin and line tin with 4 bacon rashers.

3 Melt butter in a frying pan over a medium heat, add onion and cook for 2-3 minutes or until soft. Add kidneys and cook for 2-3 minutes or until they just change colour. Stir in brandy, thyme and green peppercorns and cook, stirring, for 5 minutes or until brandy reduces by half. Set aside to cool.

4 Place lamb, breadcrumbs, stock cube, tomato paste (purée), egg and kidney mixture in a bowl and mix to combine. Spoon lamb mixture into prepared loaf tin, lay remaining bacon rashers on top and cover with aluminium foil. Place tin in a baking dish with enough boiling water to come halfway up the sides of the tin and bake for 45 minutes. Remove foil, drain off juices and bake for 45 minutes longer or until meatloaf is cooked.

5 To make sauce, place sugar and butter in a frying pan and cook over a medium heat, stirring, for 3-4 minutes or until sugar dissolves. Stir in wine, brandy, chicken stock and green peppercorns, bring to simmering and simmer for 5 minutes or until sauce reduces and thickens. Whisk in cream, bring back to simmering and simmer for 2-3 minutes longer. Serve with meatloaf.

Serves 8

Lamb and Kidney Loaf

Wellington Bread Loaf

Oven temperature
180°C, 350°F, Gas 4

1 Vienna bread loaf
30 g/1 oz butter, melted
250 g/8 oz liver pâté
125 g/4 oz button mushrooms, sliced
750 g/1 1/2 lb lean beef mince
2 tablespoons snipped fresh chives
2 teaspoons crushed black peppercorns
2 eggs, lightly beaten
1/2 beef stock cube
1 tablespoon tomato paste (purée)

RED WINE AND THYME SAUCE
30 g/1 oz butter
2 tablespoons flour
1/2 cup/125 mL/4 fl oz beef stock
1/2 cup/125 mL/4 fl oz dry red wine
freshly ground black pepper

1 Cut base from bread loaf and reserve. Scoop bread from centre of loaf leaving a 1 cm/1/2 in shell. Make bread from centre into crumbs and set aside. Brush inside of bread shell with butter, spread with pâté, then press mushroom slices into pâté.

2 Place 1 cup/60 g/2 oz reserved breadcrumbs (keep remaining breadcrumbs for another use), beef, chives, black peppercorns, eggs, stock cube and tomato paste (purée) in a bowl and mix to combine.

3 Spoon beef mixture into bread shell, packing down well. Reposition base and wrap loaf in aluminium foil. Place loaf on a baking tray and bake for 1 1/2 hours or until meat mixture is cooked.

4 To make sauce, melt butter in a saucepan over a medium heat, stir in flour and cook, stirring, for 1 minute. Remove pan from heat and gradually whisk in stock and wine. Return pan to heat and cook, stirring constantly, for 4-5 minutes or until sauce boils and thickens. Serve sauce with meatloaf.

Serves 8

Breadcrumbs are easy to make, simply place the bread in a food processor and process to make crumbs, if you do not have a food processor rub the bread through a sieve. Breadcrumbs should be made with stale bread; for this recipe either use a loaf of bread that is a day or two old or scoop out the centre of the loaf as described in the recipe, then spread the bread out on a tray and leave for 2-3 hours to become stale, before making into crumbs.

Mint Glazed Lamb Loaves

Oven temperature
180°C, 350°F, Gas 4

500 g/1 lb lean lamb mince
1/4 cup/45 g/1 1/2 oz burghul (cracked wheat), cooked and drained
1 tablespoon chopped fresh mint
1 egg, lightly beaten
1/2 chicken stock cube
freshly ground black pepper

WHEAT AND MINT FILLING
1/3 cup/60 g/2 oz burghul (cracked wheat)
1/2 cup/30 g/1 oz breadcrumbs, made from stale bread
3 tablespoons finely chopped fresh parsley
1 tablespoon finely chopped fresh mint
1 teaspoon finely grated lemon rind
1 tablespoon pine nuts, toasted
2 teaspoons mint jelly
1 apple, cored, peeled and grated
15 g/1/2 oz butter, melted

MINT GLAZE
3 tablespoons mint jelly
2 tablespoons orange juice
1 tablespoon maple syrup or honey

1 Place lamb, cooked burghul (cracked wheat), mint, egg, stock cube and black pepper to taste in a food processor and process to combine. Divide mixture into four portions and press into rectangles each measuring 10 x 15 cm/4 x 6 in.

2 To make filling, place burghul (cracked wheat) in a bowl cover with boiling water and set aside to stand for 15 minutes. Drain and rinse under cold water. Squeeze burghul (cracked wheat) to remove excess water and place in a bowl. Add breadcrumbs, parsley, mint, lemon rind, pine nuts, mint jelly, apple, butter and black pepper to taste and mix to combine.

3 Divide filling between meat rectangles and spread to cover surface, leaving a 2 cm/3/4 in border. Roll up meat like a Swiss roll and pinch ends together to seal. Place rolls, seam side down in a lightly greased baking dish.

4 To make glaze, place mint jelly in a saucepan and heat for 3-4 minutes or until jelly melts. Stir in orange juice and maple syrup or honey and cook for 1-2 minutes longer. Brush rolls with glaze and bake, brushing with glaze several times, for 35-40 minutes or until cooked.

Serves 4

For easy rolling up of meatloaves such as this one, shape the meat rectangles on pieces of plastic food wrap or aluminium foil, then use it to help roll the meat.

Glazed Family Meatloaf, Mint Glazed Lamb Loaves

GLAZED FAMILY MEATLOAF

500 g/1 lb lean beef mince
500 g/1 lb sausage meat
2 onions, finely chopped
1 cup/60 g/2 oz breadcrumbs, made from stale bread
2 teaspoons curry powder
1 teaspoon ground cumin
1 tablespoon chopped fresh parsley
1 egg, lightly beaten
1/2 cup/125 mL/4 fl oz evaporated milk
1/2 cup/125 mL/4 fl oz beef stock
freshly ground black pepper
2 tablespoons slivered almonds

TOMATO GLAZE

1/2 cup/125 mL/4 fl oz beef stock
1/3 cup/90 mL/3 fl oz tomato sauce
1 teaspoon instant coffee powder
3 tablespoons Worcestershire sauce
1 1/2 tablespoons vinegar
1 1/2 tablespoons lemon juice
1/4 cup/45 g/1 1/2 oz brown sugar
60 g/2 oz butter

1 Place beef, sausage meat, onions, breadcrumbs, curry powder, cumin, parsley, egg, evaporated milk, stock and black pepper to taste in bowl and mix to combine. Press mixture into a lightly greased 11 x 21 cm/4 1/2 x 8 1/2 in loaf tin and bake for 40 minutes. Drain off juices and turn meatloaf onto a lightly greased baking tray.

2 To make glaze, place stock, tomato sauce, coffee powder, Worcestershire sauce, vinegar, lemon juice, sugar and butter in a saucepan and bring to the boil over a medium heat. Reduce heat and simmer, stirring frequently, for 8-10 minutes or until glaze reduces and thickens slightly. Pour glaze over meatloaf, sprinkle with almonds and bake, basting frequently with glaze, for 40 minutes.

Serves 8

Oven temperature
180°C, 350°F, Gas 4

For a plain meatloaf simply omit the curry powder from the meat mixture.

Italian Sausage and Pork Roll

Oven temperature
180°C, 350°F, Gas 4

500 g/1 lb lean pork mince
250 g/8 oz Italian sausages, casings removed
1 onion, chopped
1/2 chicken stock cube
2 slices white bread, crusts removed
2 tablespoons tomato paste (purée)
1 egg, lightly beaten
freshly ground black pepper
250 g/8 oz ricotta cheese, drained
2 tablespoons chopped fresh basil
4 slices pancetta or bacon, chopped
1 red pepper, roasted and sliced
60 g/2 oz peperoni sausage, chopped
4 black olives, sliced
4 canned anchovy fillets, chopped
2 hard-boiled eggs, quartered
1 tablespoon olive oil
2 tablespoons brown sugar
1 teaspoon dried fennel seeds
1/2 teaspoon dried rosemary

1 Place pork, sausage meat, onion, stock cube, bread, tomato paste (purée), egg and black pepper to taste in a food processor and process to combine. Press out meat mixture on a large piece of aluminium foil to form a 20 x 30 cm/8 x 12 in rectangle.

2 Spread meat with ricotta cheese and sprinkle with basil. Then top with pancetta or bacon, red pepper, peperoni, olives, anchovies and hard-boiled eggs. Roll up like a Swiss roll and wrap in foil. Place on a baking tray and bake for 40 minutes. Remove foil and drain off juices.

3 Place unwrapped roll back on baking tray and brush with oil. Combine sugar, fennel seeds and rosemary, sprinkle over roll and bake for 40 minutes longer or until cooked.

Serves 6

Of Italian origin pancetta is a type of bacon available from the delicatessen section of your supermarket or Italian food shops.

Barbecue It

Barbecues are a great way to entertain family and friends, but don't limit your choice to just steak and chops. This selection of imaginative recipes will give you new ideas for your next barbecue and have everyone asking for more.

Beef with Mustard Butter

1 kg/2 lb lean rump steak in one piece and 5 cm/2 in thick, trimmed of all visible fat

LAMB AND HERB STUFFING

125 g/4 oz lean minced lamb
1/4 cup/15 g/1/2 oz breadcrumbs, made from stale bread
1 tablespoon sultanas
2 spring onions, finely chopped
1 clove garlic, crushed
1 tablespoon pine nuts, toasted
2 teaspoons finely chopped fresh rosemary
2 teaspoons finely chopped fresh mint
1 tablespoon chopped fresh parsley
2 tablespoons grated fresh Parmesan cheese
15 g/1/2 oz butter
freshly ground black pepper

MUSTARD BUTTER

60 g/2 oz butter, softened
2 tablespoons wholegrain mustard
1 tablespoon lemon juice
2 teaspoons finely chopped fresh rosemary

1 To make stuffing, heat a nonstick frying pan over a medium heat, add lamb and cook, stirring, for 4 minutes or until meat changes colour. Remove pan from heat, drain off juices and set aside to cool for 10 minutes.

2 Place lamb, breadcrumbs, sultanas, spring onions, garlic, pine nuts, rosemary, mint, parsley, Parmesan cheese, butter and black pepper to taste in a bowl and mix to combine.

3 Make a pocket in the steak by inserting a knife into one side and making a deep, wide cut. Fill pocket with lamb mixture and secure opening with wooden toothpicks or cocktail sticks. Cook steak on a lightly oiled preheated medium barbecue for 10 minutes each side or until cooked to your liking.

4 To make Mustard Butter, place butter, mustard, lemon juice and rosemary in a bowl and beat until smooth. Serve steak topped with Mustard Butter.

Serves 6-8

Don't save this recipe just for the barbecue when baked it is also excellent. To bake, prepare as described in the recipe, then place in a baking dish and bake in a preheated oven at 200°C/400°F/Gas 6 for 30-45 minutes or until cooked to your liking.

Beef with Mustard Butter

Carpetburgers with Caper Mayonnaise

500 g/1 lb lean beef mince
250 g/8 oz sausage meat
4 spring onions, finely chopped
2 cloves garlic, crushed
2 teaspoons finely grated lemon rind
1 teaspoon finely chopped fresh dill
18 bottled oysters
3 rashers bacon, cut in half lengthwise and rind removed
2 tablespoons red wine
2 tablespoons olive oil

CAPER MAYONNAISE
2 tablespoons mayonnaise
1/2 cup/125 mL/4 fl oz cream (double)
2 teaspoons chopped capers
1 teaspoon finely grated lemon rind
1 small gherkin, finely chopped

1 Place beef, sausage meat, spring onions, garlic, lemon rind and dill in a bowl and mix to combine. Shape mixture into twelve patties.

2 Top half the patties with 3 oysters each, then with remaining patties. Pinch edges of patties together to join and to completely seal the filling. Wrap a piece of bacon around each pattie and secure with wooden toothpicks or cocktail sticks.

3 Place wine and oil in a large shallow glass or ceramic dish and mix to combine. Add patties and marinate for 10 minutes.

4 Drain patties and cook on a preheated medium barbecue for 5-7 minutes each side or until cooked.

5 To make mayonnaise, place mayonnaise, cream, capers, lemon rind and gherkin in a bowl and mix to combine. Serve with patties.

Serves 6

A more economical, but just as tasty variation on that old favourite Carpetbag Steak. Prunes, dried apricots or sliced cheese can be used in place of the oysters.

Plate *Accoutrement* Napkin *In Residence*

Lamb Sausages in Pitta Pockets

Lamb Sausages in Pitta Pockets

250 g/8 oz lean lamb mince
250 g/8 oz sausage meat
1 onion, finely chopped
2 cloves garlic, finely chopped
2 tablespoons finely chopped fresh mint
2 tablespoons finely chopped fresh parsley
2 teaspoons finely grated lemon rind
1 egg white, lightly beaten
freshly ground black pepper
2 small cucumbers, chopped
1 clove garlic, crushed
250 g/8 oz natural yogurt
1 tablespoon finely chopped fresh mint
6 pitta bread ovals

1 Place lamb, sausage meat, onion, chopped garlic, mint, parsley, lemon rind, egg white and black pepper to taste in a bowl and mix to combine. Shape mixture into six thick sausages.

2 Cook sausages, turning frequently, on a lightly oiled preheated medium barbecue for 15-20 minutes or until cooked. Place cucumbers, crushed garlic, yogurt, mint and black pepper to taste in a bowl and mix to combine.

3 Top each pitta bread oval with a sausage, then with a spoonful of yogurt mixture. Serve immediately.

Serves 6

When shaping minced meat, dampen your hands and work on a lightly floured or dampened surface – this will prevent the mince from sticking to your hands and the surface.

JUMBO LAMB BURGER

500 g/1 lb lean lamb mince
1 clove garlic, crushed
1 onion, finely chopped
2 tablespoons finely chopped fresh mint
2 tablespoons finely chopped fresh parsley
1 small fresh green chilli, finely chopped
1 egg, lightly beaten
2 thick precooked 30 cm/12 in pizza bases
3 tablespoons horseradish cream
60 g/2 oz grated mozzarella cheese
60 g/2 oz grated tasty cheese (mature Cheddar)
1 large tomato, sliced

TABBOULEH

1/2 cup/90 g/3 oz burghul (cracked wheat)
1 bunch fresh parsley, chopped
1 onion, chopped
2 tablespoons olive oil
1 1/2 tablespoons lemon juice
2 cloves garlic, crushed
freshly ground black pepper

1 To make tabbouleh, place burghul (cracked wheat) in a bowl, cover with boiling water and set aside to stand for 15 minutes. Drain, then squeeze to remove excess liquid. Place burghul (cracked wheat), parsley, onion, oil, lemon juice, garlic and black pepper to taste in a bowl and mix to combine.

2 Place lamb, garlic, onion, mint, parsley, chilli and egg in a bowl and mix to combine. Press lamb mixture into a lightly greased 30 cm/12 in pizza tray, cover with aluminium foil and cook on a preheated medium barbecue for 10 minutes. Remove foil, drain off juices and cook, uncovered, for 5-10 minutes longer or until meat is cooked.

3 Place pizza bases onto a preheated medium barbecue and cook for 3-4 minutes each side or until lightly toasted. To assemble burger, turn meat pizza out of tray and place on a pizza base, then spread with horseradish cream and sprinkle with mozzarella cheese and tasty cheese (mature Cheddar). Top with tomato slices, tabbouleh and remaining pizza base. Serve cut into wedges.

Serves 6

Jumbo Lamb Burger

Chilli Malaysian Sausages

1 tablespoon peanut (groundnut) oil
1 onion, finely chopped
2 cloves garlic, crushed
1/2 teaspoon finely grated fresh ginger
1 teaspoon minced red chilli
2 tablespoons chopped fresh coriander
1 teaspoon ground cumin
500 g/1 lb lean beef mince
freshly ground black pepper
3 spring onions, finely chopped
4 large potatoes, cooked and mashed
flour
1 egg, beaten with 2 tablespoons milk
2 cups/250 g/8 oz dried breadcrumbs

CHILLI SAUCE
1 teaspoon minced red chilli
2 tablespoons sugar
2 tablespoons white wine vinegar
1 tablespoon sultanas
1 clove garlic, crushed
1/4 teaspoon soy sauce
1/4 teaspoon finely grated fresh ginger

1 Heat oil in a large frying pan over a medium heat, add onion, garlic, ginger and chilli and cook, stirring, for 2-3 minutes or until onion is soft. Stir in coriander, cumin, beef and black pepper to taste and cook, stirring, for 5 minutes or until meat is brown. Remove pan from heat and set aside to cool.

2 Add spring onions to meat mixture and mix to combine. Place a spoonful of mashed potato in one hand, flatten slightly, then place a tablespoon of meat mixture in the centre. Mould potato around meat to form an oval shape. Repeat with remaining mashed potato and meat mixture.

3 Place flour, egg mixture and breadcrumbs in separate shallow dishes. Roll sausages in flour, then dip in egg mixture and coat with breadcrumbs. Place sausages on a plate lined with plastic food wrap and chill for 30 minutes.

4 To make sauce, place chilli, sugar, vinegar, sultanas, garlic, soy sauce and ginger in a saucepan, bring to the boil, then reduce heat and simmer for 3-4 minutes or until sultanas are soft.

5 Cook sausages on a lightly oiled preheated medium barbecue plate (griddle) for 5 minutes each side or until golden brown. Serve with Chilli Sauce.

Serves 4

Make these spicy sausages up to a day in advance and store, covered, in the refrigerator until you are ready to cook them. Beef mince is used in this recipe, however, the sausages are delicious when made with pork, lamb, chicken or turkey mince.

TRADITIONAL FAVOURITES

In this chapter you will find updated versions of old favourites. Scotch Eggs are now Spicy Egg Balls and have a distinctly Oriental taste when coated with sesame seeds and flavoured with cumin and coriander. While spaghetti and meatballs have never tasted so good as when served with a sun-dried tomato sauce.

THREE-MEAT PIZZA

Oven temperature
220°C, 425°F, Gas 7

This meat-lovers' pizza is just as delicious made using one variety of mince. For a complete meal serve with a tossed green salad.

1 large eggplant (aubergine), sliced
salt
olive oil
125 g/4 oz lean beef mince
125 g/4 oz lean lamb mince
125 g/4 oz lean pork mince
3 slices salami, chopped
3 tablespoons chopped bottled pimiento or roasted red pepper
freshly ground black pepper
125 g/4 oz blue cheese, crumbled
250 g/8 oz ricotta cheese, drained
1 tablespoon finely chopped fresh basil or 1 teaspoon dried basil
1 packaged 30 cm/12 in pizza base
3 tablespoons pine nuts
3 tablespoons grated fresh Parmesan cheese

1 Sprinkle eggplant (aubergine) slices with salt and stand for 30 minutes. Rinse and pat dry with absorbent kitchen paper. Heat a nonstick frying pan over a medium heat, brush eggplant (aubergine) slices with oil and cook for 3-4 minutes each side or until golden. Remove aubergine (eggplant) from pan and set aside.

2 Heat 2 tablespoons oil in pan, add beef, lamb and pork and cook for 5 minutes or until meats are brown. Remove pan from heat and stir in salami, pimiento or red pepper and black pepper to taste.

3 Place blue cheese, ricotta cheese and basil in a bowl, mix to combine and spread over pizza base. Top with meat mixture and eggplant (aubergine) slices. Sprinkle with pine nuts and Parmesan cheese and drizzle with a little oil. Bake for 15 minutes, then reduce oven temperature to 190°C/375°F/Gas 5 and bake for 10 minutes longer.

***Serves* 6**

Three-Meat Pizza

Spicy Egg Balls

250 g/8 oz lean beef mince
250 g/8 oz sausage meat
2 tablespoons finely chopped fresh coriander
2 cloves garlic, crushed
1 teaspoon ground cumin
freshly ground black pepper
8 hard-boiled eggs
flour
1 egg, lightly beaten
2 tablespoons milk
2 cups/250 g/8 oz dried breadcrumbs
2 tablespoons sesame seeds
vegetable oil for deep-frying

PEANUT SAUCE
1 tablespoon peanut (groundnut) oil
1 small onion, finely chopped
1 clove garlic, crushed
1/2 teaspoon finely grated fresh ginger
1 cup/250 mL/8 fl oz coconut milk
1 tablespoon lime juice
4 tablespoons crunchy peanut butter
pinch of chilli powder

1 Place beef, sausage meat, coriander, garlic, cumin and black pepper to taste in bowl and mix to combine. Set aside.

2 Toss hard-boiled eggs in flour. Divide meat mixture into eight portions. Using floured hands mould one portion of meat around each egg.

3 Place beaten egg and milk in a shallow dish and whisk to combine. Place breadcrumbs and sesame seeds in a separate shallow dish and mix to combine. Dip meat-coated eggs in egg mixture, then roll in breadcrumb mixture to coat. Place on a plate lined with plastic food wrap and refrigerate for 30 minutes.

4 Heat vegetable oil in a large saucepan until a cube of bread dropped in browns in 50 seconds. Cook prepared eggs a few at a time for 7-10 minutes or until golden and cooked through. Drain on absorbent kitchen paper and keep warm.

5 To make sauce, heat peanut (groundnut) oil in a saucepan over a medium heat, add onion, garlic and ginger and cook, stirring, for 2-3 minutes or until onion is soft. Stir in coconut milk, lime juice, peanut butter and chilli powder and cook, stirring constantly, until heated and well blended. Serve with Spicy Egg Balls.

Serves 4

This recipe is a variation on the old favourite Scotch Eggs. For something different use pork mince instead of beef. Just as good cold, these Spicy Egg Balls are great picnic food and leftovers are popular for packed lunches.

TRADITIONAL LASAGNE

Oven temperature
190°C, 375°F, Gas 5

1 tablespoon olive oil
2 rashers bacon, chopped
1 large onion, chopped
1/2 red pepper, finely chopped
1 stalk celery, chopped
2 cloves garlic, crushed
500 g/1 lb lean beef mince
1 tablespoon finely chopped fresh basil or 1 teaspoon dried basil
1/4 teaspoon dried rosemary
440 g/14 oz canned tomatoes, undrained and mashed
2 tablespoons tomato paste (purée)
1/2 cup/125 mL/4 fl oz red wine
1/4 cup/60 mL/2 fl oz beef stock
1/2 teaspoon sugar
freshly ground black pepper
375 g/12 oz fresh lasagne
125 g/4 oz mozzarella cheese, grated
60 g/2 oz grated fresh Parmesan cheese
1/2 cup/125 mL/4 fl oz cream (double)

RICOTTA CHEESE SAUCE

300 g/9 1/2 oz ricotta cheese, drained
1/4 cup/60 g/2 oz sour cream
2 eggs
1/4 teaspoon ground nutmeg
125 g/4 oz tasty cheese (mature Cheddar), grated

1 Heat oil in a nonstick frying pan over a medium heat, add bacon, onion, red pepper, celery and garlic and cook, stirring, for 4-5 minutes or until onion is soft. Stir in beef and cook for 5 minutes or until meat is brown.

2 Stir basil, rosemary, tomatoes, tomato paste (purée), wine, stock and sugar into pan and bring to the boil. Reduce heat and simmer, stirring occasionally, for 30 minutes. Season to taste with black pepper.

3 Cook pasta in boiling water in a large saucepan following packet directions. Drain and place in a bowl of cold water until ready to use.

4 To make sauce, place ricotta cheese, sour cream, eggs, nutmeg and tasty cheese (mature Cheddar) in a bowl and mix combine.

5 Drain lasagne and place one-third in the base of a greased shallow ovenproof dish. Top with half the meat mixture, half the mozzarella cheese and half the sauce. Repeat layers to use all ingredients, ending with a layer of lasagne. Sprinkle with Parmesan cheese and bake for 25 minutes. Pour cream over lasagne and bake for 10-15 minutes longer or until top is golden.

Serves 6

Perfect for casual entertaining; all this tasty lasagne needs to make a complete meal is a tossed green salad or a sauté of mixed fresh vegetables and crusty bread.

Chicken Cannelloni

8 sheets fresh lasagne
30 g/1 oz butter
500 g/1 lb lean chicken mince
185 g/6 oz chicken livers, cleaned and chopped
3 slices pancetta or bacon, chopped
100 g/3 1/2 oz mozzarella cheese
2 tablespoons grated fresh Parmesan cheese

SAFFRON SAUCE

30 g/1 oz butter
1 spring onion, finely chopped
1 clove garlic, crushed
pinch saffron powder
1 cup/250 mL/8 fl oz cream (double)
1/2 cup/125 mL/4 fl oz chicken stock
pinch cayenne pepper

1 Cook pasta in boiling water in a large saucepan for 5 minutes. Drain and place in a bowl of cold water until ready to use.

2 Melt butter in a frying pan over a medium heat, add chicken and cook, stirring, for 5 minutes or until chicken changes colour. Push chicken to one side of pan, add livers and pancetta or bacon and cook, stirring, for 3-4 minutes longer. Remove pan from heat and set aside to cool.

3 Drain lasagne and pat dry with absorbent kitchen paper. Stir mozzarella and Parmesan cheeses into chicken mixture. Place heaped spoonfuls of chicken mixture down centre of each lasagne sheet and roll up. Place rolls side by side, seam side down in a greased, shallow ovenproof dish. Set aside.

4 To make sauce, melt butter in a saucepan, add spring onion and garlic and cook, stirring, for 3 minutes. Stir in saffron powder and cook for 1 minute longer. Add cream, stock and cayenne pepper, bring to the boil, then reduce heat and simmer, stirring occasionally, for 8 minutes or until sauce thickens slightly.

5 Pour sauce over rolls, cover and bake for 20 minutes or until heated through.

Serves 4

Oven temperature
180°C, 350°F, Gas 4

Make this easy dish up to a day in advance and store, covered in the refrigerator until you are ready to bake and serve it. For a complete meal serve with a salad of mixed lettuce and herbs or steamed green vegetables such as beans, asparagus or snow peas (mangetout) and crusty bread or rolls.

Chicken Cannelloni

Plate Villeroy & Boch

Pork and Apple Cabbage Rolls

Oven temperature
180°C, 350°F, Gas 4

2 tablespoons vegetable oil
1 onion, finely grated
2 rashers bacon, chopped
1 green apple, peeled, cored and grated
1 teaspoon caraway seeds
500 g/1 lb lean pork mince
125 g/4 oz brown rice, cooked
1 egg, lightly beaten
freshly ground black pepper
8 large cabbage leaves
60 g/2 oz butter
1 1/2 tablespoons paprika
1 1/2 tablespoons flour
1 tablespoon tomato paste (purée)
1/2 cup/125 mL/4 fl oz red wine
1 1/2 cups/375 mL/12 fl oz chicken stock
1/2 cup/125 g/4 oz sour cream

1 Heat oil in a frying pan over a medium heat, add onion and bacon and cook, stirring, for 3-4 minutes or until onion is soft. Stir in apple and caraway seeds and cook for 2 minutes longer. Remove pan from heat and set aside to cool.

2 Place pork, rice, egg, black pepper to taste and onion mixture in a bowl and mix to combine.

3 Boil, steam or microwave cabbage leaves until soft. Refresh under cold running water, pat dry with absorbent kitchen paper and trim stalks.

4 Divide meat mixture between cabbage leaves and roll up, tucking in sides. Secure with wooden toothpicks or cocktail sticks.

5 Melt 30 g/1 oz butter in a frying pan, add rolls and cook, turning several times, until lightly browned. Transfer rolls to a shallow ovenproof dish.

6 Melt remaining butter in pan over a medium heat, stir in paprika and flour and cook for 2 minutes. Stir in tomato paste (purée), wine and stock and bring to the boil. Reduce heat and simmer, stirring, for 5 minutes. Remove pan from heat and whisk in sour cream. Pour sauce over rolls, cover and bake for 1 hour.

Serves 4

These rolls are delicious if made using lamb mince instead of the pork. This recipe is a good way to use up leftover cooked rice and spinach or silverbeet leaves can be used instead of cabbage.

Crunchy Cottage Pie

Oven temperature
180°C, 350°F, Gas 4

Any mince or combination of minces can be used to make this tasty cottage pie. The pie is almost a meal in itself, all you need for a complete meal are steamed green vegetables such as zucchini (courgettes), beans or cabbage.

1 tablespoon olive oil
1 onion, finely chopped
1 clove garlic, crushed
125 g/4 oz mushrooms, sliced
2 rashers bacon, chopped
500 g/1 lb lean beef mince
3 tablespoons tomato sauce
1 1/2 tablespoons Worcestershire sauce
1 teaspoon soy sauce
1 3/4 cup/440 mL/14 fl oz beef stock
1/4 teaspoon dried thyme
2 tablespoons chopped fresh parsley
freshly ground black pepper

CRUNCHY VEGETABLE TOPPING
3 large potatoes, chopped
250 g/8 oz pumpkin or carrots, chopped
1 egg, lightly beaten
1/4 cup/60 g/2 oz sour cream
1/4 teaspoon nutmeg
1/4 cup/30 g/1 oz chopped pumpkin seeds (pepitas)
1/4 cup/30 g/1 oz dried breadcrumbs
30 g/1 oz grated fresh Parmesan cheese
60 g/2 oz butter, melted

1 Heat oil in a frying pan over a medium heat, add onion and cook, stirring, for 1 minute. Add garlic, mushrooms and bacon and cook, stirring constantly, for 2 minutes. Stir in beef and cook for 5 minutes or until meat is brown.

2 Stir tomato sauce, Worcestershire sauce, soy sauce, stock, thyme, parsley and black pepper to taste into pan. Bring to simmering and simmer, uncovered, for 25-30 minutes or until mixture reduces and thickens. Spoon meat mixture into an ovenproof pie dish.

3 To make topping, place potatoes, pumpkin or carrots, egg, sour cream and nutmeg in a bowl and mix to combine. Spoon vegetable mixture over meat mixture. Place pumpkin seeds (pepitas), breadcrumbs, Parmesan cheese and butter in a bowl and mix to combine. Sprinkle over vegetable mixture and bake for 45 minutes or until meat mixture is hot and bubbling and topping is golden.

Serves 4

Crunchy Cottage Pie

Plates *The Bay Tree*

Middle Eastern Meatballs

Middle Eastern Meatballs

500 g/1 lb lean beef mince
60 g/2 oz couscous, cooked
1 teaspoon ground allspice
2 tablespoons chopped fresh parsley
1 egg, lightly beaten
flour
60 g/2 oz ghee or butter
2 cups/500 mL/16 fl oz beef stock
1 cinnamon stick
2 tablespoons honey
1/4 teaspoon saffron powder
1/2 teaspoon ground nutmeg
3 tablespoons sultanas
3 tablespoons chopped dried apricots
2 tablespoons fruit chutney
1/4 cup/60 mL/2 fl oz orange juice
2 teaspoons grated orange rind
30 g/1 oz blanched almonds, toasted

1 Place beef, couscous, allspice, parsley and egg in a bowl and mix to combine. Shape into small balls, coat with flour and set aside.

2 Heat ghee or butter in a large saucepan and cook meatballs in batches, for 5 minutes or until brown on all sides. Return meatballs to pan, pour in stock, add cinnamon stick and bring to boil. Reduce heat and simmer for 10 minutes.

3 Stir honey, saffron, nutmeg, sultanas, apricots and chutney into pan, cover and simmer for 30 minutes. Stir in orange juice and simmer, uncovered, for 10 minutes longer or until liquid reduces and thickens slightly. Serve sprinkled with orange rind and almonds.

Serves 4

These meatballs look great served on a bed of saffron rice or couscous. To make saffron rice, soak a few strands of saffron in 3 tablespoons warm water and add to water when cooking the rice. Instead of saffron you can use 1/4 teaspoon ground turmeric, in which case there is no need to soak it; simply add to the water and rice.

Lamb with Blue Cheese Topping

Oven temperature
180°C, 350°F, Gas 4

250 g/8 oz lean lamb mince
2 cloves garlic, crushed
2 teaspoons yellow mustard seeds
2 spring onions, chopped
1 thick slice white bread, crusts removed
1 egg white, lightly beaten
2 tablespoons pistachio nuts, chopped
4 lean racks lamb, each containing 3 cutlets
2 tablespoons vegetable oil
125 g/4 oz blue cheese, crumbled
30 g/1 oz butter, softened
2 teaspoons port or red wine
1 tablespoon chopped fresh parsley

PORT SAUCE
1/2 cup/125 mL/4 fl oz chicken stock
1/2 cup/170 g/5 1/2 oz cranberry sauce
3 tablespoons redcurrant jelly
1 tablespoon port or red wine
1 teaspoon yellow mustard seeds
freshly ground black pepper

For a milder flavour use cream cheese in this recipe instead of blue cheese; almonds are a good alternative to pistachio nuts.

1 Place lamb mince, garlic, mustard seeds, spring onions, bread and egg white in a food processor and process to combine. Fold in pistachio nuts.

2 Using a sharp knife, separate bones from meat on lamb racks, leaving both ends intact, to make pockets. Fill pockets with lamb mixture and place racks in a heatproof baking dish. Brush racks with oil and bake for 30 minutes.

3 Place blue cheese, butter, port or wine and parsley in a bowl and mix to combine. Spread cheese mixture over back of each rack and bake for 15-20 minutes or until topping is brown. Remove racks from baking dish, place on a serving platter, set aside and keep warm.

4 To make sauce, place baking dish over a medium heat, add stock, cranberry sauce, redcurrant jelly, port or wine, mustard seeds and black pepper to taste and bring to the boil, stirring. Reduce heat and simmer for 5 minutes or until sauce reduces and thickens slightly. Serve sauce with lamb racks.

Serves 4

Remember the more cutting and preparation meat has had, the shorter the storage life, so mince will not keep as long as chops or steaks. If possible buy mince on the day you intend to use it and never keep longer than 2 days before using.

New Spaghetti and Meatballs

500 g/1 lb lean beef mince
1 onion, finely chopped
1 clove garlic, crushed
1 tablespoon finely chopped fresh basil or 1 teaspoon dried basil
4 slices Italian salami, finely chopped
2 teaspoons tomato paste (purée)
1 egg, lightly beaten
flour
2 tablespoons olive oil
250 g/8 oz spaghetti
60 g/2 oz grated fresh Parmesan cheese

SUN-DRIED TOMATO SAUCE
30 g/1 oz butter
1 clove garlic, crushed
4 slices proscuitto or ham, chopped
2 tablespoons chopped fresh rosemary or 1 teaspoon dried rosemary
1/2 cup/125 mL/4 fl oz chicken stock
1/2 cup/125 mL/4 fl oz red wine
16 sun-dried tomatoes in olive oil, drained and chopped
freshly ground black pepper
2 tablespoons chopped fresh basil

1 Place beef, onion, garlic, basil, salami, tomato paste (purée) and egg in a bowl and mix to combine. Shape mixture into small balls and roll in flour.

2 Heat oil in a large frying pan over a medium heat and cook meatballs in batches, for 5 minutes or until brown on all sides. Remove meatballs from pan and set aside.

3 To make sauce, wipe pan clean, add butter and melt over a medium heat. Add garlic, proscuitto or ham and rosemary and cook for 2 minutes. Stir in stock and wine and return meatballs to pan. Bring to the boil, then reduce heat and simmer for 15 minutes. Stir in sun-dried tomatoes and black pepper to taste and continue to cook until sauce reduces slightly. Remove pan from heat and stir in basil.

4 Cook pasta in boiling water in a large saucepan following packet directions. Drain well. To serve, spoon meatballs and sauce over hot spaghetti and sprinkle with Parmesan cheese.

Serves 4

When shaping minced meat, dampen you hands and work on a lightly floured or dampened surface – this prevents the mince from sticking to your hands and the work surface. An egg added to mince mixtures binds them and makes them easier to shape.

New Spaghetti and Meatballs

Chilli Meat Pattie Casserole

Oven temperature
200°C, 400°F, Gas 6

500 g/1 lb lean beef mince
2 tablespoons taco seasoning mix
1 egg
3/4 cup/45 g/1 1/2 oz breadcrumbs, made from stale bread
250 g/8 oz tasty cheese (mature Cheddar), grated
vegetable oil
1 onion, finely chopped
1 small fresh red chilli, finely chopped
2 cloves garlic, crushed
440 g/14 oz canned tomatoes, undrained and mashed
1/2 cup/125 mL/4 fl oz bottled tomato salsa
1 1/2 tablespoons tomato paste (purée)

HASH BROWN TOPPING
2 large potatoes, scrubbed
2 eggs, lightly beaten
155 g/5 oz packet corn chips, crushed

1 Place beef, taco seasoning mix, egg, breadcrumbs and half the cheese in a bowl and mix to combine. Shape meat mixture into eight patties.

2 Heat 2 tablespoons oil in a nonstick frying pan over a medium heat, add patties and cook for 3-4 minutes each side or until brown. Place patties in a shallow ovenproof dish and set aside.

3 Heat 1 tablespoon oil in pan over a medium heat, add onion, chilli and garlic and cook, stirring, for 3-4 minutes or until onion is soft. Stir in tomatoes, salsa and tomato paste (purée) and bring to the boil. Reduce heat and simmer for 5 minutes. Pour sauce over meat patties.

4 To make topping, boil, steam or microwave potatoes until just tender. Drain and refresh under cold running water. Peel potatoes and grate coarsely. Place potatoes, eggs and corn chips in a bowl and mix to combine.

5 Heat 2 tablespoons oil a large frying pan over a medium heat and cook spoonfuls of potato mixture for 3-4 minutes each side or until golden. Remove from pan, drain on absorbent kitchen paper and place slightly overlapping, on top of patties, sprinkle with remaining cheese and bake for 40 minutes.

Serves 4

Sure to be popular with children, serve this casserole with a tossed green salad or steamed green vegetables such as beans or cabbage to make a complete meal.

White plate *Villeroy & Boch*

Chilli Meat Pattie Casserole

BologNESE Authentico

1 tablespoon olive oil
2 rashers bacon, chopped
2 onions, chopped
2 cloves garlic, crushed
1 small carrot, finely chopped
1 celery stalk, finely chopped
500 g/1 lb lean beef mince
250 g/8 oz lean pork mince
125 g/4 oz chicken livers, chopped
1/4 teaspoon ground nutmeg
freshly ground black pepper
1/2 cup/125 mL/4 fl oz dry white wine
2 cups/500 mL/16 fl oz beef stock
1 1/2 tablespoons tomato paste (purée)
1 tablespoon chopped fresh basil
1 tablespoon chopped fresh parsley
1/2 cup/125 mL/4 fl oz cream (double)
750 g/1 1/2 lb pasta of your choice, cooked

1 Heat oil in a large saucepan over a medium heat, add bacon, onions, garlic, carrot and celery and cook, stirring, for 3-4 minutes or until onions are soft. Remove vegetable mixture from pan and set aside.

2 Add beef, pork, chicken livers, nutmeg and black pepper to taste to pan and cook over a medium heat, stirring, for 5 minutes or until meats are brown. Return vegetable mixture to pan and stir in wine. Bring to the boil and boil until almost all the liquid has evaporated.

3 Stir stock and tomato paste (purée) into meat mixture, bring to the boil, then reduce heat and simmer, stirring occasionally, for 30-35 minutes.

4 Stir in basil, parsley and cream and cook over a low heat for 1-2 minutes. To serve, spoon over hot pasta.

Serves 6

Bolognese sauce is an all-time favourite to serve with spaghetti. Other pastas such as penne, fettuccine and pappardelle are also good choices. The bolognese can be made using just beef mince if you wish.

WRAP IT UP

In this chapter you will find exciting ways to turn mince into something really special that family and friends will love.

CHICKEN, LEEK AND POTATO PIE

Oven temperature
220°C, 425°F, Gas 7

1 egg, lightly beaten with
1 tablespoon water

CHEESE PASTRY
60 g/2 oz cream cheese, softened
75 g/2½ oz tasty cheese (mature Cheddar), grated
125 g/4 oz butter, softened
1½ cups/185 g/6 oz flour, sifted
3 tablespoons sesame seeds
2 egg yolks

LEEK AND CHICKEN FILLING
60 g/2 oz butter
3 leeks, sliced
375 g/12 oz lean chicken mince
1 chicken stock cube
freshly ground black pepper
1 large potato, cooked and sliced
½ cup/125 mL/4 fl oz cream (double)
¼ cup/60 mL/2 fl oz chicken stock
1 egg, lightly beaten
3 tablespoons snipped fresh chives

1 To make pastry, place cream cheese, tasty cheese (mature Cheddar) and butter in a bowl and beat until soft and creamy. Mix in flour, sesame seeds and egg yolks to make a stiff dough. Turn dough onto a lightly floured surface and knead briefly. Wrap in plastic food wrap and refrigerate for 30 minutes.

2 To make filling, melt butter in a frying pan over a medium heat, add leeks and cook, stirring, for 3-4 minutes or until soft. Stir in chicken and cook for 4-5 minutes longer or until chicken changes colour. Stir in stock cube and black pepper to taste. Set aside to cool.

3 Roll out two-thirds of the pastry and use to line the base and sides of a 20 cm/ 8 in springform cake tin. Line with nonstick baking paper and fill with uncooked rice. Bake for 10 minutes, then remove rice and paper and bake for 10 minutes longer or until pastry is golden. Set aside to cool.

4 Spread half the chicken mixture over base of pastry shell, then top with half the potato slices. Repeat layers, finishing with a layer of potato. Combine cream, stock, egg and chives and pour over chicken.

5 Roll out remaining pastry large enough to cover pie. Brush rim of pastry shell with egg mixture and place pastry lid over filling, gently press edges together to seal then trim to neaten. Brush pie top with egg mixture. Make slits in top of pie using a small shape knife and bake for 15 minutes. Reduce temperature to 190°C/ 375°F/Gas 5 and bake for 30 minutes.

Serves 6

Great hot, warm or cold, this pie is a spectacular dish for a special picnic. When minced chicken is unavailable buy skinless, boneless chicken breast or thigh fillets and mince it yourself, alternatively you can use a whole chicken or chicken pieces, these will take a little more preparation as you will need to remove the skin and bones before mincing.

Chicken, Leek and Potato Pie

Sweet Pork Buns

Oven temperature
220°C, 425°F, Gas 7

BUN DOUGH

30 g/1 oz fresh yeast, crumbled or
1 3/4 teaspoons active dry yeast
1/4 cup/60 mL/2 fl oz lukewarm water
60 g/2 oz butter
1 cup/250 mL/8 fl oz milk
1/4 cup/60 g/2 oz sugar
2 eggs, lightly beaten
1 teaspoon salt
3 3/4 cups/470 g/15 oz flour, sifted

PORK FILLING

2 teaspoons peanut (groundnut) oil
250 g/8 oz lean pork mince
1 clove garlic, crushed
1/2 teaspoon finely grated fresh ginger
1 tablespoon hoisin sauce
1 tablespoon oyster sauce
2 tablespoons soy sauce
1/2 teaspoon sesame oil
3 teaspoons cornflour blended with
1/2 cup/125 mL/4 fl oz chicken stock
3 spring onions, finely chopped
1 egg, lightly beaten with
1 tablespoon water

GLAZE

1/4 cup/60 g/2 oz sugar
1/3 cup/90 mL/3 fl oz water

1 To make dough, place yeast and water in a bowl and whisk with a fork until yeast dissolves. Set aside in a warm draught-free place for 5 minutes or until foamy. Place butter and milk in a saucepan and cook over a medium heat, stirring constantly, until butter melts. Remove pan from heat and set aside until lukewarm. Pour milk mixture into yeast mixture, then stir in sugar, eggs and salt and beat to combine. Stir in flour and beat vigorously until mixture is smooth and satiny. Cover bowl with plastic food wrap and set aside in a warm draught-free place for 40 minutes or until doubled in volume.

2 To make filling, heat oil in a frying pan over a medium heat, add pork, garlic and ginger and cook, stirring, for 5 minutes or until meat is brown. Stir in hoisin sauce, oyster sauce, soy sauce, sesame oil and cornflour mixture and bring to the boil. Reduce heat and simmer for 5 minutes or until mixture thickens. Remove pan from heat, add spring onions and set aside to cool.

3 Turn dough onto a floured surface and knead for 10 minutes or until dough is smooth and no longer sticky. Roll dough out to 1 cm/1/2 in thick and using a 5 cm/2 in cutter, cut out twelve rounds.

4 Using your index finger make an indent in centre of half the dough rounds. Place a spoonful of filling in each indent. Brush remaining dough rounds with egg mixture and place over rounds with filling. Pinch edges together firmly and

There are two types of yeast commonly used in baking – fresh and dried. Dried yeast works as well as fresh but takes longer to activate. It is twice as concentrated as fresh yeast, so you will require half as much. You will find that 15 g/1/2 oz dried yeast has the same rising power as 30 g/1 oz fresh yeast. Fresh yeast is also known as baker's or compressed yeast.

place buns on a greased baking tray, cover and set aside in a warm draught-free place for 30 minutes or until almost doubled in size. Bake for 10 minutes, then reduce temperature to 200°C/400°F/Gas 6 and bake for 5 minutes longer or until buns are golden.

5 To make glaze, place sugar and water in a saucepan and cook over a medium heat, stirring constantly, without boiling until sugar dissolves. Bring to boil, then boil rapidly until mixture becomes syrupy. Set aside to cool slightly. Brush warm buns with glaze.

Makes 6

Beef and Egg Pies

Oven temperature
220°C, 425°F, Gas 7

When you are making a pie with a cooked filling it is important that the filling is cold before you place it in the pie dish and top with the pastry lid. If the filling is hot or warm it will cause the pastry to go tough and soggy.

750 g/1 1/2 lb prepared shortcrust pastry
375 g/12 oz prepared puff pastry
1 egg, lightly beaten with
1 tablespoon water

BEEF FILLING
1 tablespoon vegetable oil
1 onion, chopped
2 rashers bacon, chopped
375 g/12 oz lean beef mince
1 tablespoon flour
1/2 teaspoon dried thyme
1/4 cup/60 mL/2 fl oz tomato sauce
1 tablespoon Worcestershire sauce
1 cup/250 mL/8 fl oz beef stock
2 teaspoons cornflour blended with
1 tablespoon water
freshly ground black pepper
8 eggs
125 g/4 oz grated tasty cheese
(mature Cheddar)

1 To make filling, heat oil in a frying pan over a medium heat, add onion and bacon and cook, stirring, for 3-4 minutes. Stir in beef and cook for 5 minutes or until meat is brown. Add flour and thyme and cook, stirring constantly, for 2 minutes. Stir in tomato sauce, Worcestershire sauce, stock, cornflour mixture and black pepper to taste and bring to the boil. Reduce heat and simmer for 5 minutes or until mixture thickens. Remove pan from heat and set aside to cool.

2 Line base and sides of eight greased small metal pie dishes with shortcrust pastry. Divide filling between pie dishes. Using the back of a spoon, make a depression in the centre of filling mixture and carefully slide an egg into each hollow. Sprinkle with cheese.

3 Cut rounds of puff pastry to fit tops of pies. Brush edges of shortcrust pastry with water, then top with puff pastry. Press edges together to seal. Brush with egg mixture, make two slits in the top of each pie and bake for 20-25 minutes or until golden.

Makes 8

Beef and Egg Pies

Four-Cheese Calzone

30 g/1 oz butter
1 onion, sliced
250 g/8 oz lean chicken mince
375 g/12 oz prepared puff pastry
125 g/4 oz ricotta cheese, drained
125 g/4 oz mozzarella cheese, sliced
4 slices Italian salami, chopped
3 canned artichokes, drained and sliced
freshly ground black pepper
60 g/2 oz tasty cheese (mature Cheddar), grated
45 g/1 1/2 oz grated fresh Parmesan cheese
1 egg, lightly beaten with 1 tablespoon water

1 Melt butter in a frying pan over a medium heat, add onion and cook for 3-4 minutes or until soft. Remove onion from pan and set aside. Add chicken to pan and cook for 3-4 minutes or until it changes colour.

2 Roll out pastry to 5 mm/1/4 in thick and cut out a 30 cm/12 in round. Spread ricotta cheese over pastry round, leaving a 2 cm/3/4 in border around the edge. Top one half of pastry with mozzarella cheese, onion, chicken, salami, artichokes and black pepper to taste. Combine tasty cheese (mature Cheddar) and Parmesan cheese and sprinkle three-quarters of the mixture over filling.

3 Brush border of pastry round with egg mixture, fold uncovered side over filling, rolling edges to seal, then crimp or flute to make a neat and decorative border.

4 Place calzone on a lightly greased baking tray, brush with egg mixture, sprinkle with remaining cheese mixture and bake for 20-25 minutes or until puffed and golden. Stand for 5-10 minutes before serving.

Serves 4

Oven temperature
220°C, 425°F, Gas 7

A calzone is basically a pizza folded over to encase the filling. Because the filling is sealed in during baking it is much more succulent. This easy variation only needs a tossed green salad to make a complete meal.

Four-Cheese Calzone

Spicy Lamb Rolls

Oven temperature
220°C, 425°F, Gas 7

1 tablespoon olive oil
1 onion, finely chopped
315 g/10 oz lean lamb mince
1 tablespoon tomato paste (purée)
2 teaspoons honey
1/4 teaspoon ground cinnamon
1/2 teaspoon ground allspice
2 teaspoons finely chopped fresh mint
2 teaspoons lemon juice
1/2 teaspoon finely grated lemon rind
1 tablespoon pine nuts
16 sheets filo pastry
125 g/4 oz butter, melted

1 Heat oil in a frying pan over a medium heat, add onion and cook for 2-3 minutes or until soft.

2 Add lamb, tomato paste (purée), honey, cinnamon, allspice, mint, lemon juice and lemon rind to pan and cook, stirring, for 5 minutes or until meat is brown. Remove pan from heat and set to cool. Stir in pine nuts.

3 Layer 4 sheets of pastry, brushing each with melted butter. Cut pastry in half, lengthways, then cut each half into quarters. Place a spoonful of meat mixture on one edge of each pastry piece and roll up, tucking in sides to make a thin roll. Repeat with remaining pastry and filling.

4 Place rolls on a baking tray, brush with remaining butter and bake for 10-15 minutes or until pastry is golden and filling cooked.

Serves 4

If you do not have a food processor mix the mince and other ingredients together in a bowl, the texture will not be as fine but the result and taste will be just as good. For a finer texture purchase fine minced lamb or mince it again yourself before preparing the rolls.

Devilled Corn Muffins

Oven temperature
200°C, 400°F, Gas 6

Corn meal (polenta) is cooked yellow maize flour and is very popular in northern Italian cooking. Polenta refers to both the name of a dish and the yellow maize flour.

2 cups/250 g/8 oz self-raising flour, sifted
2/3 cup/125 g/4 oz corn meal (polenta)
2 tablespoons sugar
pinch cayenne pepper
3 tablespoons chopped bottled pimiento or roasted red pepper
90 g/3 oz tasty cheese (mature Cheddar), grated
125 g/4 oz butter, melted
3/4 cup/185 mL/6 fl oz milk
2 eggs, lightly beaten

DEVILLED BEEF FILLING
1 tablespoon vegetable oil
250 g/8 oz lean beef mince
1 teaspoon curry powder
2 tablespoons brown sugar
2 tablespoons tomato sauce
2 teaspoons Worcestershire sauce
1 teaspoon soy sauce
2 teaspoons lemon juice

Makes 12

1 To make filling, heat oil in a frying pan over a medium heat, add beef and cook, stirring, for 5 minutes or until meat is brown. Stir in curry powder and brown sugar and cook for 2 minutes longer. Mix in tomato sauce, Worcestershire sauce, soy sauce and lemon juice and bring to the boil. Reduce heat and simmer for 10 minutes or until mixture thickens. Set aside to cool.

2 Place flour, corn meal (polenta), sugar, cayenne pepper, pimiento or red pepper and cheese in a bowl and mix to combine. Stir in butter, milk and eggs and mix until just combined.

3 Half fill lightly greased muffin tins with corn meal (polenta) mixture, then top with a heaped teaspoonful of filling and enough corn meal (polenta) mixture to almost fill the tins. Bake for 20-25 minutes or until muffins are cooked when tested with a skewer.

Crispy Chilli Turnovers

When handling fresh chillies do not put your hands near your eyes or allow them to touch your lips. To avoid discomfort and burning, wear rubber gloves. Freshly minced chilli is also available in jars from supermarkets.

500 g/1 lb prepared puff pastry
vegetable oil for deep-frying

SPICY BEEF FILLING
30 g/1 oz ghee or butter
500 g/1 lb lean beef mince
1 onion, finely chopped
2 teaspoons finely grated fresh ginger
2 cloves garlic, crushed
1 small fresh green or red chilli, finely chopped
1/2 teaspoon ground turmeric
1/2 teaspoon ground cumin
1/2 teaspoon garam masala
freshly ground black pepper
1/2 cup/125 mL/4 fl oz beef stock
1 tablespoon lime or mango chutney

1 To make filling, melt ghee or butter in a large frying pan over a medium heat, add beef and cook, stirring, for 5 minutes. Stir in onion, ginger, garlic, chilli, turmeric, cumin, garam masala and black pepper to taste and cook until onion is soft.

2 Stir stock and chutney into meat mixture and bring to the boil. Reduce heat and simmer for 20 minutes or until most of the liquid evaporates. Remove pan from heat and set aside to cool.

3 Roll out pastry on a lightly floured surface to 5 mm/1/4 in thick and using a 7.5 cm/3 in cutter cut out rounds.

4 Place a spoonful of the meat mixture in the centre of each pastry round. Brush edges lightly with water and fold pastry over filling. Press edges together, then pinch with your thumb and index finger. Fold pinched edges over and pinch again.

5 Heat oil in a large saucepan until a cube of bread dropped in browns in 50 seconds and cook a few turnovers at a time for 3-4 minutes or until filling is cooked and pastry golden.

Serves 6

Devilled Corn Muffins, Crispy Chilli Turnovers

HEALTHY IDEAS

In times past mince, has had the reputation of being fatty. Today you will find that every supermarket and butcher has lean mince, so just because you are watching what you eat, you need not exclude mince from the menu. This selection of tasty recipes will delight the health-conscious and is sure to be popular with the family.

SAUSAGE AND ROAST PEPPER SALAD

125 g/4 oz penne, cooked and cooled
2 red peppers, roasted and cut into strips
2 yellow or green peppers, roasted and cut into strips
125 g/4 oz button mushrooms, sliced
155 g/5 oz pitted black olives
5 English spinach leaves, stalks removed and leaves finely chopped

HERBED BEEF SAUSAGES
500 g/1 lb lean beef mince
185 g/6 oz sausage meat
2 cloves garlic, crushed
1 teaspoon chopped fresh rosemary
1 tablespoon finely chopped fresh basil
2 slices proscuitto or lean ham, finely chopped
1 tablespoon olive oil
freshly ground black pepper

HERB DRESSING
1/2 cup/125 mL/4 fl oz olive oil
1/4 cup/60 mL/2 fl oz balsamic or red wine vinegar
2 teaspoons chopped fresh basil or 1 teaspoon dried basil
1 teaspoon chopped fresh oregano or 1/4 teaspoon dried oregano
freshly ground black pepper

1 To make sausages, place beef, sausage meat, garlic, rosemary, basil, proscuitto or ham, olive oil and black pepper to taste in a bowl and mix to combine. Shape mixture into 10 cm/4 in long sausages. Cook sausages under a preheated medium grill, turning occasionally, for 10-15 minutes or until brown and cooked through. Set aside to cool slightly, then cut each sausage into diagonal slices.

2 To make dressing, place olive oil, vinegar, basil, oregano and black pepper to taste in a screwtop jar and shake well to combine.

3 Place sausage slices, penne, red peppers, yellow or green peppers, mushrooms and olives in bowl, spoon over dressing and toss to combine. Line a serving platter with spinach leaves, then top with sausage and vegetable mixture.

Serves 4

Sausage and Roast Pepper Salad

To prevent pasta that is for use in a salad from sticking together, rinse it under cold running water immediately after draining.
All this mouth-watering salad needs to make a complete meal is some crusty bread or wholemeal rolls.

LAMB RAGOUT WITH VEGETABLES

Often thought of as a type of grain couscous is actually a pasta made from durum wheat, however cook and use it in the same way as a grain. The name couscous refers to both the raw product and the cooked dish. It is an excellent source of thiamin and iron as well as being a good source of protein and niacin.

1 cup/185 g/6 oz couscous
1 turnip, quartered
1 large carrot, quartered
1 large potato, quartered
$^1/_2$ head cauliflower, broken into large florets
1 large parsnip, quartered
1 large zucchini (courgette), quartered
1 sweet potato, quartered

LAMB RAGOUT

500 g/1 lb lean lamb mince
$^3/_4$ cup/45 g/$1^1/_2$ oz breadcrumbs, made from stale bread
3 cloves garlic, crushed
1 spring onion, finely chopped
2 tablespoons finely chopped fresh parsley
1 egg, lightly beaten
2 tablespoons olive oil
1 stalk celery, chopped
1 onion, chopped
1 tablespoon flour
$^3/_4$ cup/185 mL/6 fl oz dry white wine
1 cup/250 mL/8 fl oz chicken stock
$^1/_2$ cup/125 mL/4 fl oz tomato purée
2 teaspoons finely grated lemon rind
1 tablespoon finely chopped fresh thyme or 1 teaspoon dried thyme
315 g/10 oz canned butter beans, drained and rinsed

1 To make ragoût, place lamb, breadcrumbs, garlic, spring onion, parsley and egg in a bowl and mix to combine. Shape mixture into small meatballs. Heat 1 tablespoon oil in a large saucepan and cook meatballs in batches for 3-4 minutes or until brown.

2 Heat remaining oil in same pan, add celery and onion and cook for 3-4 minutes or until onion is soft. Stir in flour and cook, stirring, for 1-2 minutes or until flour is brown. Remove pan from heat and gradually whisk in wine, stock and tomato purée. Return pan to heat and bring to the boil. Reduce heat, add lemon rind, thyme, beans and meatballs and simmer, uncovered, for 30 minutes.

3 Place couscous in a bowl, pour over 2 cups/500 mL/16 fl oz boiling water and toss with a fork until couscous absorbs almost all the liquid.

4 Boil, steam or microwave turnip, carrot, potato, cauliflower, parsnip, zucchini (courgette) and sweet potato until tender. To serve, arrange couscous around the edge of a large serving platter, pile vegetables in the centre, then top with ragoût.

Serves 4

Considered to be the national dish of Morocco couscous is also used widely in the cuisines of Algeria and Tunisia.

MUSHROOM AND MEATBALL SOUP

An easy and nourishing soup that is just as delicious made with pork or lamb mince.

60 g/2 oz butter
1 leek, sliced
250 g/8 oz button mushrooms, sliced
2 tablespoons seasoned flour
1 1/2 cups/375 mL/12 fl oz evaporated milk
2 cups/500 mL/16 fl oz chicken stock
1/2 cup/100 g/31/2 oz natural yogurt
2 tablespoons snipped fresh chives

FRENCH ONION MEATBALLS
250 g/8 oz lean minced beef
1 tablespoon French onion soup powder
2 tablespoons breadcrumbs
1 egg, lightly beaten
1 tablespoon water
1 tablespoon vegetable oil

1 Melt butter in a large saucepan, add leek and cook for 2-3 minutes. Add mushrooms and cook for 3-4 minutes. Add flour and cook, stirring, for 1 minute.

2 Remove pan from heat and gradually stir in milk and stock. Return pan to heat and bring to the boil, stirring constantly. Reduce heat and simmer for 20 minutes.

3 To make meatballs, place beef, soup powder, breadcrumbs, egg and water in a food processor and process to combine. Shape mixture into small balls. Heat oil in a nonstick frying pan over a medium heat and cook meatballs in batches for 5 minutes or until browned and cooked through. Remove from pan and drain on absorbent kitchen paper.

4 To serve, divide meatballs between soup bowls and ladle over hot soup. Top with a spoonful of yogurt and sprinkle with chives.

Serves 4

MEATBALL AND NOODLE SOUP

A tasty Oriental-style soup that is a meal in itself. For a more substantial meal start or finish with naan bread and a salad of shredded Chinese cabbage, chopped spring onions, chopped fresh basil and coriander tossed with Oriental Dressing. To make Oriental Dressing, place 1 teaspoon sesame oil, 1 teaspoon grated fresh ginger, 2 teaspoons soy sauce, 1 tablespoon water, 1 teaspoon vinegar and 1/4 teaspoon crushed garlic, in a screwtop jar and shake well to combine.

220 g/7 oz g lean pork mince
125 g/4 oz lean chicken mince
1 egg white, lightly beaten
4 tablespoons chopped fresh coriander
1 teaspoon chilli paste (sambal oelek)
125 g/4 oz rice noodles
2 teaspoons vegetable oil
8 oyster mushrooms, stems removed
3 cups/750 mL/1 1/4 pt chicken stock
1 tablespoon lime juice
2 tablespoons fish sauce
1 tablespoon brown sugar
1 carrot, cut into thin strips
3 spring onions, cut into thin strips

Serves 4

1 Place pork, chicken, egg white, 2 tablespoons fresh coriander and chilli paste (sambal oelek) in a food processor and process to combine. Shape mixture into small balls and steam or microwave until cooked. Set aside.

2 Place noodles in a bowl, pour over boiling water to cover and set aside to stand for 8 minutes. Drain well. Heat oil in a large saucepan, add mushrooms and cook for 2 minutes. Stir in stock, lime juice, fish sauce and sugar, bring to the boil and boil for 5 minutes. Stir in carrot and spring onions and cook for 1 minute. Divide meatballs and noodles between soup bowls, ladle over hot soup and sprinkle with remaining coriander.

Mushroom and Meatball Soup, Meatball and Noodle Soup

MEDITERRANEAN FRITTATA

Oven temperature
180°C, 350°F, Gas 4

Serve frittata hot, warm or cold, cut into wedges, accompanied by a tossed green salad and crusty bread or rolls.

1 tablespoon olive oil
1 red onion, sliced
250 g/8 oz lean beef mince
2 slices pancetta or bacon, cut into strips
2 cloves garlic, crushed
2 tablespoons finely chopped fresh basil
60 g/2 oz sun-dried tomatoes, sliced
60 g/2 oz black olives, chopped
2 potatoes, cooked and sliced
6 eggs, lightly beaten
60 g/2 oz grated fresh Parmesan cheese
freshly ground black pepper

1 Heat oil in a large frying pan over a medium heat, add onion and cook, stirring, for 3-4 minutes or until onion is soft. Remove onion from pan and set aside. Add beef, pancetta or bacon and garlic to pan and cook, stirring, for 5 minutes or until meat is brown. Drain off cooking juices.

2 Stir basil, sun-dried tomatoes and olives into meat mixture and spoon into a greased 20 cm/8 in pie dish. Top with onions and potatoes.

3 Place eggs, Parmesan cheese and black pepper to taste in a bowl and whisk to combine. Pour egg mixture over meat mixture and bake for 20-25 minutes or until frittata is set.

Serves 6

Left: Mediterranean Frittata
Above: Meatball and Bean Salad

Meatball and Bean Salad

1 onion, chopped
1 clove garlic, crushed
1/2 teaspoon chilli powder
2 teaspoons ground cumin
500 g/1 lb lean beef mince
2 tablespoons tomato paste (purée)
60 g/2 oz tasty cheese (mature Cheddar), grated
1 slice white bread, crusts removed
1 egg white, lightly beaten
1 tablespoon canola or olive oil
2 x 440 g/14 oz canned three bean mix, drain and rinsed
250 g/8 oz yellow teardrop or cherry tomatoes

CHILLI DRESSING

1/4 cup/60 mL/2 fl oz vegetable oil
1 1/2 tablespoons red wine vinegar
1/4 cup/60 mL/2 fl oz bottled tomato salsa
1/2 teaspoon sugar
1/2 teaspoon bottled minced chilli
2 tablespoons chopped fresh parsley

1 Place onion, garlic, chilli powder, cumin, beef, tomato paste (purée), cheese, bread and egg white in a food processor and process to combine. Shape mixture into small balls.

2 Heat oil in a nonstick frying pan over a medium heat and cook meatballs in batches for 4-5 minutes or until brown and cooked through. Drain on absorbent kitchen paper.

3 To make dressing, place oil, vinegar, salsa, sugar, chilli and parsley in a screwtop jar and shake well to combine.

4 Place meatballs, beans and tomatoes in a large salad bowl. Spoon over dressing and toss to combine.

Serves 4

Canola oil is the oil extracted from the rape plant, a member of the cabbage family. It differs from traditional rapeseed oil in that it does not contain the high levels of erucic acid. This has made rape a vaulable crop, as consumption of large quantities of eruric acid by humans has been shown to cause changes to heart muscles.
In recent years canola oil has become increasing popular due to the predominance of mono-unsaturated fats in it.
Canned three bean mix as used in this recipe is a mixture of butter beans, red kidney beans and lima beans. Any canned mixed beans are suitable to use.

RAVIOLI WITH CORIANDER PESTO

500 g/1 lb fresh lasagne
flour

LAMB FILLING
315 g/10 oz lean lamb mince
1 clove garlic, crushed
1 tablespoon grated fresh Parmesan cheese
1 teaspoon finely chopped fresh coriander
$^{1}/_{4}$ teaspoon ground nutmeg
freshly ground black pepper

CORIANDER PESTO
1 large bunch fresh coriander
2 cloves garlic, crushed
60 g/2 oz pine nuts
60 g/2 oz grated fresh Parmesan cheese
$^{1}/_{2}$ cup/125 mL/4 fl oz olive oil

1 To make filling, place lamb, garlic, Parmesan cheese, coriander, nutmeg and black pepper to taste in a bowl and mix to combine.

2 Place teaspoons of filling 5 cm/2 in apart over half the lasagne sheets. Brush edges and between filling lightly with water and top with remaining lasagne sheets. Press firmly between fillings and along edges and cut into squares using a pastry wheel. Sprinkle ravioli with a little flour.

3 Cook ravioli in boiling water in a large saucepan for 5 minutes, or until just tender. Drain well.

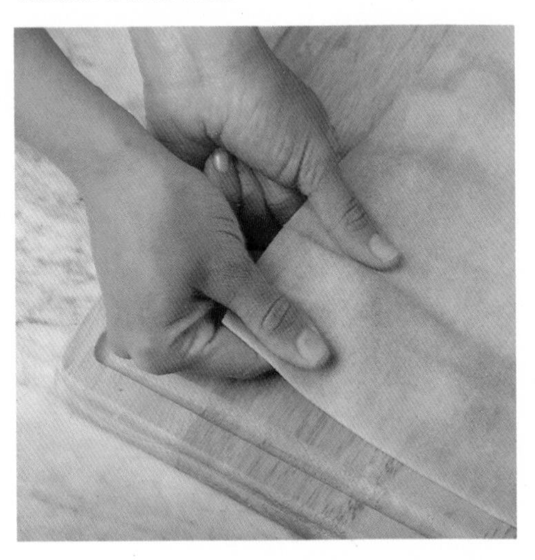

4 To make pesto, place coriander leaves, garlic, pine nuts and Parmesan cheese in a food processor and process to finely chopped. With machine running, slowly pour in oil and process until smooth. Serve with ravioli.

Serves 4

An easy yet different mince dish that is just as delicious made with pork, chicken or turkey mince. If you wish make the ravioli and pesto up to a day in advance and store it covered in the refrigerator.

Beef with Prawns and Noodles

Beef with Prawns and Noodles

155 g/5 oz rice noodles
1 tablespoon peanut (groundnut) oil
2 cloves garlic, crushed
250 g/8 oz lean beef mince
250 g/8 oz uncooked prawns, shelled and deveined
2 tablespoons caster sugar
2 tablespoons white vinegar
1 tablespoon fish sauce
1 fresh red chilli, finely chopped
2 eggs, lightly beaten
125 g/4 oz bean sprouts
1 large carrot, grated
3 tablespoons chopped fresh coriander
2 tablespoons chopped blanched almonds

1 Place noodles in a bowl, pour over boiling water to cover and set aside to stand for 8 minutes. Drain well.

2 Heat oil and garlic in a wok or large frying pan over a high heat, add beef and stir-fry for 2-3 minutes or until meat is brown. Add prawns and stir-fry for 1 minute. Stir in sugar, vinegar, fish sauce, and chilli and bring to boil, stirring constantly.

3 Add eggs to pan and cook, stirring, until set. Add bean sprouts, carrot and noodles and toss to combine. To serve, sprinkle with coriander and almonds.

Serves 4

For a more economical dish omit the prawns and increase the quantity of mince to 500 g/1 lb, alternatively you can use canned prawns.

Spicy Sausage with Vegetables

HEALTHY

500 g/1 lb lean beef mince
2 cloves garlic, crushed
75 g/2$^1/_2$ oz desiccated coconut
1 tablespoon tomato paste (purée)
2 tablespoons chopped fresh coriander
1 small carrot, grated
2 teaspoons ground cumin
$^1/_4$ cup/60 mL/2 fl oz coconut milk
2 teaspoons curry powder
2 eggs, lightly beaten

VEGETABLE SAUCE
1 tablespoon peanut (groundnut) oil
1 clove garlic, crushed
1 teaspoon finely grated fresh ginger
2 carrots, cut into thin strips
1 red pepper, cut into thin strips
155 g/5 oz snow peas (mangetout), trimmed
4 asparagus spears, cut into 5 cm/2 in lengths
30 g/1 oz bean sprouts
$^1/_4$ cup/60 mL/2 fl oz chicken stock
1 tablespoon oyster sauce
$^1/_4$ teaspoon ground cumin

1 Place beef, garlic, coconut, tomato paste (purée), coriander, carrot, cumin, coconut milk, curry powder and eggs into a food processor and process to combine. Shape beef mixture into 10 cm/4 in long sausages.

2 Place sausages under a preheated medium grill and cook, turning frequently, for 10-15 minutes or until cooked through and golden. Remove sausages from grill and set aside to cool slightly, then cut each into diagonal slices.

3 To make sauce, place oil, garlic and ginger in a wok or large frying pan and stir-fry over a medium heat for 1 minute. Add carrots, red pepper, snow peas (mangetout), asparagus and bean sprouts and stir-fry for 2-3 minutes longer.

4 Stir stock, oyster sauce and cumin into vegetable mixture and cook, stirring, for 3-4 minutes or until sauce thickens and vegetables are tender. Add sausage slices, toss to combine and cook for 1 minute longer or until heated through.

Serves 4

Serve this delicious stir-fry on a bed of boiled brown rice or noodles. Any mince can be used to make the sausages, for something different you might like to try chicken or pork mince.

Spicy Sausage with Vegetables

Beef-filled Golden Nuggets

Oven temperature
180°C, 350°F, Gas 4

4 golden nugget pumpkins
2 teaspoons peanut (groundnut) oil

BEEF AND LENTIL FILLING
30 g/1 oz ghee or butter
1 onion, finely chopped
1 clove garlic, crushed
1 teaspoon ground cumin
1 teaspoon ground coriander
1 teaspoon ground cardamom
1 teaspoon ground turmeric
250 g/8 oz lean beef mince
1 small parsnip, peeled and sliced
100 g/3 1/2 oz red lentils
440 g/14 oz canned whole tomatoes, undrained and mashed
1/2 cup/125 mL/4 fl oz beef stock
1 teaspoon chilli paste (sambal oelek)
freshly ground black pepper

1 Cut a 2.5 cm/1 in lid from each pumpkin and set aside. Scoop seeds out of pumpkins and discard. Brush inside and skin of each pumpkin with oil and place on a baking tray. Brush lids with oil, place on pumpkins and bake for 30 minutes.

2 To make filling, melt ghee or butter in a large saucepan over a medium heat, add onion and garlic and cook for 2-3 minutes or until onion is soft. Stir in cumin, coriander, cardamom and turmeric and cook for 2 minutes longer. Add beef and cook, stirring, for 5 minutes or until meat is brown.

3 Stir parsnip, lentils, tomatoes and stock into meat mixture and bring to the boil. Reduce heat, cover and simmer for 15 minutes. Add chilli paste (sambal oelek) and black pepper to taste and cook, stirring occasionally, for 15 minutes or until lentils are tender and mixture thickens.

4 Spoon filling into pumpkins, cover with lids and bake for 30 minutes or until pumpkins are tender.

Serves 4

These beef and bean-filled pumpkins are delicious served with coleslaw and natural low-fat yogurt. For a change use the filling with other vegetables such as peppers.

Beef-filled Potatoes

Oven temperature
180°C, 350°F, Gas 4

This recipe is a good way of using leftover cold meat. Simply mince the leftover meat and use in place of the beef mince. Any mince or meat is suitable to use.
For a quicker version of this dish cook the potatoes in the microwave on HIGH (100%) for 10-15 minutes or until tender.

6 large old potatoes, scrubbed
1/4 cup/60 mL/2 fl oz canola or olive oil

MUSHROOM FILLING
30 g/1 oz butter
1 onion, finely chopped
1 clove garlic, crushed
250 g/8 oz button mushrooms, sliced
250 g/8 oz lean beef mince
1 tablespoon tomato paste (purée)
250 g/8 oz low-fat natural yogurt
60 g/2 oz reduced-fat Cheddar cheese

1 Pierce potatoes several times with a skewer and bake for 1 hour or until tender. Cut potatoes in half and scoop out flesh, leaving a 1 cm/1/2 in thick shell. Place flesh in a bowl, mash and reserve. Brush potatoes inside and out with oil and place on a baking tray, cut side up.

2 To make filling, melt butter in a frying pan over a medium heat, add onion and garlic and cook for 2 minutes. Stir in mushrooms and cook for 2 minutes longer. Add beef and cook, stirring, for 5 minutes or until meat is brown. Remove pan from heat, stir in tomato paste (purée) and yogurt.

3 Add meat mixture to mashed potato and mix to combine. Spoon filling into potato shells, sprinkle with cheese and bake for 15 minutes or until top is golden.

Serves 6

Sweet Potato and Pork Crumble

Oven temperature
180°C, 350°F, Gas 4

For something different make this recipe using pumpkin instead of sweet potatoes. You will need 750 g-1 kg/ 1 1/2-2 lb pumpkin.

30 g/1 oz butter
1/4 cup/60 mL/2 fl oz orange juice
1 tablespoon honey
1 tablespoon brown sugar
1 teaspoon finely grated fresh ginger
2 sweet potatoes, cooked and sliced
1 tablespoon vegetable oil
1 clove garlic, crushed
1 teaspoon ground cinnamon
250 g/8 oz lean pork mince
1/4 cup/60 mL/2 fl oz tomato purée
1 tablespoon port or red wine

PECAN CRUMBLE
1 cup/60 g/2 oz wholemeal breadcrumbs, made from stale bread
1/2 cup/45 g/1 1/2 oz rolled oats
1/2 cup/90 g/3 oz brown sugar
1 teaspoon ground cinnamon
60 g/2 oz butter
60 g/2 oz chopped pecans

Serves 4

1 Melt butter in a frying pan over a medium heat, stir in orange juice, honey, brown sugar and ginger and cook for 2-3 minutes or until mixture is syrupy. Add sweet potatoes and toss to coat. Set aside.

2 Heat oil in a clean frying pan over a medium heat, add garlic and cinnamon and cook for 1 minute. Add pork and cook, stirring, for 5 minutes. Stir in tomato purée and port or wine, bring to the boil, then reduce heat and cook for 8 minutes or until most of the liquid evaporates. Place half the sweet potatoes in the base of a greased shallow ovenproof dish, top with pork mixture, then remaining sweet potatoes.

3 To make crumble, combine breadcrumbs, rolled oats, brown sugar and cinnamon in a bowl. Rub in butter and stir in pecans. Sprinkle over meat mixture and bake for 40 minutes.

Beef-filled Potatoes, Sweet Potato and Pork Crumble

Lamb Ratatouille and Egg Bake

Oven temperature
180°C, 350°F, Gas 4

olive oil
315 g/10 oz lean lamb mince
1 clove garlic, crushed
3 canned anchovy fillets, drained and finely chopped
4 eggs
3 tablespoons chopped black olives
60 g/2 oz chorizo sausage, sliced
60 g/2 oz grated tasty cheese (mature Cheddar)

RATATOUILLE

1 large eggplant (aubergine), cut into 2.5 cm/1 in pieces
salt
1 large onion, chopped
1 clove garlic, crushed
1 red pepper, chopped
3 zucchini (courgettes), sliced
440 g/14 oz canned tomatoes, undrained and mashed
freshly ground black pepper

1 To make Ratatouille, place eggplant (aubergine) in a colander set over a bowl, sprinkle with salt and set aside to stand for 30 minutes. Rinse under cold running water and pat dry with absorbent kitchen paper.

2 Heat 2 tablespoons oil in a saucepan over a medium heat, add onion and garlic and cook for 2 minutes. Stir in eggplant (aubergine) and red pepper and cook for 3 minutes longer. Add zucchini (courgettes), tomatoes and black pepper to taste and bring to the boil. Reduce heat, cover and simmer for 10-15 minutes or until eggplant (aubergine) is soft. Remove pan from heat and set aside.

3 Heat 1 tablespoon oil in a frying pan over a medium heat, add lamb and cook, stirring, for 5 minutes or until it changes colour. Stir in garlic and anchovies and cook for 2 minutes longer. Transfer meat mixture to a shallow ovenproof dish and spoon over Ratatouille mixture. Using the back of a tablespoon make four depressions in top of mixture and slide an egg into each depression. Top with olives, chorizo sausage and cheese and bake for 15-20 minutes or until eggs are cooked.

Serves 4

Chorizo sausage is a spicy sausage, if it is unavailable use any spicy sausage or salami instead.

INDEX